FRANKLIN ISLAND

FRANKLIN ISLAND

A Novel

America's 250th Anniversary Edition

MICHAEL LAPIERRE

DEDICATION

This book is dedicated to the memory of those dive-bombing waterfowl on Franklin Island, from 1913 to 1918, who gave their lives so that Lola and the rest of the Clinch family members could exquisitely, sumptuously consume their delicacies at the supper table.

However, with great respect and watch-care over the birds on the island, that responsible father and lighthouse keeper extraordinaire, Albert J. Clinch, insisted that his family be kind, gentle, swift, and only harvest those particular life-sustaining waterfowl the Clinch family would eat that same evening, and those that were of the proper size, girth, and age. These birds were a wonderful blessing to the Clinch family, and their memory lives on throughout this book!

A special note of dedication also goes out to the U.S. Fish and Wildlife Service and the Franklin Island Wildlife Refuge for their unwavering commitment to protecting the stunningly beautiful 12-acre wildlife habitat on the island.

The Franklin Island Lighthouse is remembering earlier times and more vibrant days. She especially remembers those rascal little Clinch children from 1913 to 1918! (Photo by Bob Trapani, Jr.)

CONTENTS

FOREWORD

THERE ARE STORIES THAT ENTERTAIN AND STORIES THAT TAKE you home. Franklin Island is the latter. In these pages, Michael LaPierre invites us into the life of a remarkable family who leave the mainland for Franklin Island, Maine—six nautical miles off the shore and a world away from the noise of modern life. The year is 1913. The automobile is still a novelty. Industry is rising. The world is changing. Yet on this small island, anchored by a lighthouse and surrounded by the steady rhythm of the sea, something timeless unfolds.

Told through the warm and perceptive voice of the oldest daughter, Lola, this story captures five formative years—1913 to 1918—of a family of eleven: a father called to serve as lighthouse keeper, a devoted mother, and nine spirited children. What follows is their own version of Swiss Family Robinson—a life rich with adventure and responsibility, hardship, and joy.

There are forts built from discarded wood and imagination. Fishing lines cast at dawn. Hunts in crisp autumn air. Igloos shaped by days of energetic work. Bicycle and ski jumps crafted from courage and youthful daring. These children are not entertained—they are engaged. They are not distracted—they are formed.

But this is more than a chronicle of childhood escapades.

It is a story about family—about siblings who become lifelong allies, about parents whose words of wisdom echo across generations. It is about faith—not as an ornament to life but as its foundation. On Franklin Island, Scripture is not merely quoted; it is lived. Work is worship. Responsibility is character-building. Loss is real, but so is hope. Joy is abundant, but it is anchored in something deeper than circumstance.

As I read this book, I found myself transported back to my own childhood—long days on my great-grandparents' farm, where time seemed slower and life seemed clearer. Those years shaped me in ways I did not fully understand until much later. The lessons learned there—about work, faith, family, and perseverance—formed the foundation of who I am today. In many ways, Franklin Island stirred those same memories and reminded me why they matter.

We often say we wish life was simpler. Yet what we truly long for is not simplicity—it is meaning. This story reminds us that meaning is not found in convenience or abundance but in connection: to family, to purpose, to God.

The world of 1913–1918 might feel distant, but the truths woven through these pages are not. The closeness of family. The shaping influence of friends. The sadness of loss. The courage required to grow up. The responsibility to carry forward a legacy of faithfulness. These are not relics of a bygone era—they are guideposts for today.

Michael LaPierre has written a heartwarming, deeply human story that every reader will recognize in some measure. Whether you grew up on a farm, in a small town, or in a bustling city, you will see yourself somewhere on Franklin Island. You will recognize the laughter. The tears. The mischief. The prayers whispered in uncertainty. The steady faith that carries a family through changing seasons.

Ultimately, this book reminds us of a profound truth: we are all living our story as part of God's greater story. Our chapters might differ in setting and circumstance, but the *Author* remains the same. And when a family chooses to live according to His Word, their legacy stretches far beyond their own years.

Franklin Island is a charming and endearing tale of a time long past—but its message is strikingly present. It reminds us not only how life was once lived but how it still can be lived: with courage, gratitude, faith, and unwavering love.

I am grateful to have walked the shores of Franklin Island through these pages. I trust you will be, too.

— Steven Nail, Dean, College of Business and Economics,
Anderson University

ACKNOWLEDGMENTS

— xiii —

ABIG THANK YOU GOES OUT TO MY FAVORITE COFFEE HOUSE IN Traveler's Rest, South Carolina, for allowing me to hang out, sip their outstanding coffee, listen to my literary updates, and write this labor of love!

As usual, Darren Shearer and his complement of highly qualified professionals at High Bridge Media are instrumental in bringing this book to market.

A heartfelt thank you also goes out to those who were able to suffer through my initial "drafts" and give me much-needed and valuable feedback. You know who you are.

I would be remiss if I didn't thank my Lord and Savior, Jesus Christ, for giving me a "special unction" of literary clarity and motivation. It is an unexpected surprise with the most curious timing. *God only knows.*

PROLOGUE

CHRISTIAN NOVELS WRITTEN TO PROCLAIM CHRIST AND SPREAD the gospel message are much needed in our culture.

Together, as people of faith, we must stand tall and help one another navigate the complexities of our society.

If we are asking American citizens at large to consider Christ and to put down their secular forms of passive mass media consumption, we must then seek to provide numerous holistic alternatives to fill that void.

We know idle minds can be a very dangerous thing.

Shall we continue to pollute the minds of our youth with secular gobbledygook or dust off the ancient manuscripts of old and embrace those authors who aspire to proclaim and rekindle the standards and principles found in God's Word?

My prayer is that teachers, parents, and students alike will find this book conducive to engaging the hearts, minds, and souls of a new generation to come.

We must put off the old and put on the new for the hope of a brighter Christ-filled tomorrow.

May God bless our great country, these states united, and the incredible citizens past and present who help make up our 250th celebration of a declared independence, leading us toward the history-altering Constitutional Republic resolution by the consent of the governed!

And, most importantly of all, to the praise of His infinite glory!

To God Be the Glory! Amen!

CAST OF CHARACTERS

Lola – She is the main character in the story and our hero! We watch a shy young Southern Maine country teenager, fraught with much insecurity, grow from a naive, inexperienced introvert into the matriarch of a family as an equal partner. Lola's persona exudes a natural self-deprecating style and always shows complete deference and respect to others when in their company.

Mom – Lola's mom (Mrs. Albert J. Clinch), and the mother of nine children, has a fiery, disciplined, and direct personality. She is both greatly loved and greatly feared.

Dad – Lola's dad (Mr. Albert J. Clinch) likes to stay in the background because of his very reserved nature, but he also exhibits deep personal growth in this story. He surprises us greatly every once in a little while. He was one of fourteen children growing up, and we suspect he is trying to break a new record!

Emile LaPierre – A likable, funny, and confident French Canadian who moved down from New Brunswick, Canada, with his mother and brother. A complex personality with some warts that need to be smoothed away.

Harold LaPierre – Emile's younger brother and a hard-working French Canadian who lets his older brother take the lead.

Mrs. LaPierre – A woman from New Brunswick, Canada, who is trying to get her life back on track with her two sons after falling on hard times. A disappointed soul who has so far experienced a very difficult life.

Big Chief – Lola's older brother (Teddy Clinch), who is the oldest child with an oversized ego. The love of attention and bravado are often in conflict with his need to be liked. He oozes charisma.

Razor – Lola's second-oldest brother (Willie Clinch), a problem child who loves the great outdoors. His enigmatic wars are internal.

Mad – Lola's younger sister (Madelynn Clinch) and the second girl to be born, who loves the finer things in life. Some folks are destined to live out the dreams manufactured in their youth.

Hocker – Lola's third younger brother (Peter Clinch), who always had a flair for business as a youngster and is Lola's favorite brother. A little humor, some optimistic and jovial conversations, and a few bright ideas can get one down the line quite a ways in business!

Reet – Lola's second younger sister (Rita Clinch), who sees the world through rose colored glasses. She is the spiritual one with much discipline and determination. Nice people can finish first!

Johnny Boy – Lola's fourth younger brother (Jonathan Clinch), who is endlessly looking for a risk-filled adventure. Some might say he is the forgotten one.

Jo-Jo – Lola's third-youngest sister (JoAnne Clinch), who is the loud and obnoxious one in the family but is loved. A rough stone that we hope one day will take form with a little polishing.

Al – Lola's fifth younger brother (Albert Clinch, Jr.), who is a real intellect and a very bright bulb. Such a rare intellectual breed!

Mr. Jedidiah Grassenpoop (pronounced Graws-sen-pop) – A successful Massachusetts businessman who becomes a close Clinch family friend and confidant. With each new event and circumstance, he grows on you.

Mrs. Isabella Grassenpoop (pronounced Graws-sen-pop) – Mr. Jed's wonderful and very patient wife who has learned to be flexible. The sweetest disposition known to mankind.

Pastor Goodlander – The Clinch family Pastor from Scarborough, Maine, who is very good at what he does and loves people. Some say Abe Lincoln reincarnated to a limited extent.

Susan Goodlander – Lola's roommate for a brief period in Gorham, Maine. A sweet young lady and a spiritual lifesaver.

Pastor Gladwell – The Clinch Family Pastor in Friendship, Maine, who is a barrel of optimism. A half-full cup forever spilling over into a reservoir of positivity.

Mrs. Gladwell – A hyper version of Pastor Gladwell, who is over-the-top friendly and outgoing. Hold on to your britches; Mrs. G has arrived!

Mr. Hockenbass – Lola's first official boss, who can be a *tad bit* prickly. Some folks have a wonderful persona and work very hard. Others don't and just work hard. Oops, did I just say that?

Mr. Leon Bean – Founder of L.L. Bean in Freeport, Maine, and a very generous man. A man with high energy, compassion, and an intuitive understanding of the pragmatism of everyday living.

Dr. Popwell – A chiropractic doctor in Friendship, Maine. A name and a vocation that are a match made in heaven.

Hammer – First Wagon Master. The French name "Martel" is translated as "Hammer" in English. He is of French-Canadian descent. A rough-edged money-making Down East Mainer with little to no manners.

Roy – Second Wagon Master. The name "Roi" is the French version of the English name Roy. He is of French-Canadian descent. In many respects, he is riding the coattails of his lifelong friend Hammer, but he doesn't know any better.

Daisy – The Clinch family dog and a perfectly placed gift during a dark and dreary period. We can't get enough of this precious *little bugger*.

Oden Moros (Translated Raging Doom) – Emile LaPierre's business partner at the oil distribution company. Sometimes we have to deal with and put up with evil for a spell, and sometimes we just run away…fast!

Lilith Ciara-Moros (Translated Dark Night Monster) – The wife of Oden Moros. Evil does have a twin!

Mr. and Mrs. Pellegrin – A very happy couple from church willing to pitch in and help during a time of crisis. It is not possible to wipe that smile off their faces.

Mary Benton – An employee at the Friendship Fish Cannery and a fellow church member. A very helpful young lady.

Janice Hightower – Another employee at the Friendship Fish Cannery and a fellow church member. Love her endless mountain of hair stacked three miles high!

John Nathan Hunter – A wise young preacher from Limington, Maine. A good ole Maine *preacher boy* just starting out.

Larry Wilcox – A friendly and very likable deacon at a church in Limington, Maine, where Lola and Emile settled down. A man who will not be forgotten.

Mr. and Mrs. Almond Twitchell – The previous lighthouse keeper and his wife on Franklin Island Lighthouse off the coast of Friendship, Maine. Thank you for your dedication to the Lighthouse Service.

Mr. McDonald – Owner of the only restaurant in Friendship, Maine. God used this small business owner to be an encouragement and unknowingly help start many generations of "righteous misfits!"

Captain Jonathan Randall Davenport III – The Captain of the ship who was instrumental during the Clinch family crisis. There are those who have class, and those who demonstrate what it's like to have "real class!"

Tom and Rosie – A sweet young couple who got caught in the raging seas of the Atlantic. The entire Clinch family came to the rescue with pleasure.

INTRODUCTION

THIS NOVEL IS WRITTEN BY MICHAEL JAMES LAPIERRE THROUGH the eyes of his grandmother, Lola May Clinch. This journey shares the romanticism, folklore, and fantasy of what it meant to be a lighthouse keeper's daughter and a Maine "islander" to boot, born and lived out in the early twentieth century on Franklin Island, Maine. It was the year of our Lord 1913.

I spent a great deal of time with my grandmother and grandfather growing up. Lola and Emile were their respective given names. They have long since passed away, though the memories of our time together are still very vivid and fresh in my mind.

In the early years of my youth, when the summer months rolled around, outside of being on a baseball diamond or basketball court, there was a very high likelihood that you would find me at my grandparents' house.

We did everything together. I mean everything! From vacations to cribbage to solitaire, to long country drives, to working on projects, to grabbing an ice cream cone or two, we enjoyed our time together and were inseparable.

Being the oldest grandchild of the family put me in a good position to "hog" all of their free time. I was their favorite grandchild, and they made no bones about telling me that fact in private.

However, from time to time, it would create quite a stir in our immediate family since equal time wasn't being shared with my other four siblings. My grandparents would try to involve my sisters and brother the best they knew how, but within a few months of addressing said complaints, I was back to spending a disproportionate amount of time with them by comparison.

As a result of my close relationship, I spent countless hours listening to their bygone childhood memories and stories and was spellbound by all of their real or misremembered "goings-on" in their youth.

The "stories" were frequent and endless, and I could not get enough. Nana's Franklin Island lighthouse recollections especially captured and piqued my restless and overactive mind and creative imagination.

My grandmother (Lola) was a true-blue born and raised Mainer who had a very unique personality and style of communication. Some would say she often butchered the King's English, although I thought it a charming and memorable part of who she was.

Lola had a plethora of key phrases, witticisms, Maine colloquialisms, often-made-up words to fit an occasion, and other common Maine expressions and superlatives she would frequently demonstrate in her conversations with others.

Some were good, some pushed the envelope *a little bit,* and others were not so good. I have chosen to use only a few in this novel, the others to remain forever silent.

She used regular phrases like *thank you, Lord, hooligans, what a blessing, don't-never-mind, high muckety-mucks, God only knows, heebie jeebies, okey-doke, you little whipper-snapper, looky here, cunin', ayuh, wicked-good, bebopping around, right-out-straight, upta camp, anyhoo, extra-most-bestest, ignoramus, throwing good money after bad, a tad-little-bit, whatchamacallit, whosawhatsit, little bugger, lobsta feed, you cahn't get they-yah from hea-yah, tell a lie, all by your lonesome, super-duper, rabble-rouser, mite bit, thingamagig,* and any other off-beat phrase used in Maine that might pop into her head at any given time.

You just never knew what she was about to come out with. Readers will find her phrases "laced" throughout this novel, which is based on the life story of an authentic, true-blooded Mainer! Oops, I almost wrote "Maineiac!" My bad!

There is no question in my mind that my grandmother was a follower of Jesus Christ, proclaimed His name, and knew Him as her personal Savior. However, there were some small conversational irregularities and abnormalities that just didn't seem to bother her in the lifelong pursuit of biblical perfection.

Yes, she was a sinner saved by the grace of God and fought the old man within and the associated sinful tugs just like you and I do.

She was an intriguing and enigmatic Mainer shaped by the times, her surroundings, events, familial ties, chance, and most importantly of all, biblical instruction.

That being said, she was the *extra-most-bestest* grandmother anyone could have, notwithstanding my grandmother on my mother's side, who passed away at an early age, so I didn't get a chance to know her all that well. From what I've heard, she too, was an *extra-most-bestest* grandparent.

With that as a backdrop, I hope you learn to love and cherish the woman I called Nana, whose name is Lola and whose childhood nickname is "Mumsy" in this work of historical drama.

While this novel (fantasy story) has been slightly embellished and polished to tell a complete and accurate Maine storyline, many of the facts are based on my grandmother's life-calling, humor, witticisms, real or imagined childhood events, and keen introspection on life itself.

May this manuscript and work of love stay consistent with Lola's unique overall persona; the imagined events that enveloped her days on God's created island lighthouse paradise; those circumstances that helped shape her robust and fulfilling life; and one that is so notably found in the Holy Scriptures.

> To everything there is a season, and a time to every
> purpose under the heaven: a time to be born and a time
> to die; a time to plant, and a time to pluck up that
> which was planted; a time to kill, and a time to heal; a
> time to break down, and a time to build up; a time to
> weep, and a time to laugh; a time to mourn, and a time
> to dance; a time to cast away stones, and a time to
> gather stones together; a time to embrace, and a time
> to refrain from embracing; a time to get, and a time to
> lose; a time to keep, and a time to cast away; a time to
> rend, and a time to sew; a time to keep silent, and a

time to speak; a time to love, and a time to hate; a time
of war and a time of peace. (Ecclesiastes 3:1-8)

I must confess that the story you are about to read possesses all
the elements found in those verses in Ecclesiastes, to the amazement
and astonishment of its author. It is uncanny!

Please, grab a cup of joe, sit back, and let your mind wander and
be taken in by the excitements, struggles, fears, laughter, wholesomeness, purity, and the divine of this manuscript. Watch Lola
grow from a shy, awkward, inexperienced teen to a confident
woman able to hold her own.

While she never ascended to positions of notoriety, fame, or so-
cietal recognition, in our family, she will always be recognized and
cherished as the quintessential soft-spoken matriarch who loved her
family and loved the Lord to the best of her ability.

As I held her hand during the last days of her life in the hospital,
I prayed a prayer out loud that expressed those exact sentiments.

She gently squeezed my hand and said, "Thank you for your
beautiful prayer."

Next, with outstretched arms and tears flowing down her
cheeks, she said, "Give me a hug."

It is now my prayer that this book inspires and motivates you
to share it with friends, family, and loved ones.

Out of respect to those family members who might still be alive,
I have changed the names of the characters in this novel, with the
exception of a few who have already passed. I have chosen to take
extra measures to protect all innocent family members!

PS: I apologize in advance if this book doesn't, in some small
and subtle way, move your range of emotions. It is designed for that
very end based on Lola's imagined life story, and I will be disappointed if I have failed to properly detail and expound on many of
her gripping life experiences.

1

SCHOOL IS OUT!

THE FIRST BREATH OF SUMMER FREEDOM HAD FINALLY ARRIVED. It was the early days of June in the cool, blustery summer of 1913 in Scarborough, Maine, where school had just been let out for another year. Anyone who had spent any time at all in beautiful, mesmerizing New England realized that the month of June could be a *hodgepodge* of weather conditions before warming up later in the summer. This year was no exception.

Brr … sweaters and jackets were certainly not optional these last few days. The Maine state birds (black flies and mosquitoes) had also been out in full complement this June in between cold spells, tormenting those of us who were fair-skinned and susceptible to these pesky and irritable little demon-like gnats.

However, this year I wouldn't let anything, demon-bugs included, stand in the way of the happiness, exhilaration, and joy I felt now that we were out of school. I was on cloud nine! I could not believe I had survived another year! Thank you, Lord!

That barn-red one-room schoolhouse in Scarborough, Maine, had been my "semi-forced" home away from home and familiar acquaintance these many years now. Here, I started to learn how to interact with other children who were not my brothers or sisters. Yes, I had brothers and sisters! Boy… did I have brothers and sisters!

I grew up in a family with nine children! I had five brothers and three sisters, and "we girls" were unfairly overmatched and unmercifully pestered. Well, I must admit I might be embellishing *a tad* because of that boy-girl and brother-sister thing we had going on.

Anyhoo, there were some days when I could let out an unmerciful and high-pitched scream!

My brothers were Teddy (Big Chief-17), who loved to talk and make everything larger than life and was a bit of a braggard; Willie (Razor-16) was always in trouble for one thing or another, but a fine outdoorsman in every respect of the word; Jonathan (Johnny Boy-10) was the apple of mother's eyes but was forever pushing the envelope in some sort of an adventure mode or just trying to be a daredevil; Albert Jr. (Al-9) was smart as a whip and loved his primer books; and Peter (Hocker-13) was the boy who knew how to turn a quick buck and my favorite brother.

The names of my sisters were Madelynn (Mad-14), who liked the finer things in life and was a bit stuck-up and a clothes hound; JoAnne (Jo-Jo-8) was out loud and always wanted to be heard, wiggling her way into anyone's conversation; Rita (Reet-12) was the peacemaker in the family who always had nice things to say about anything and everyone; and then there was me, Lola (Mumsy-15), who liked the simple things in life and just wanted to be left alone, however impossible that might be in such a ginormous family as the Clinch family.

Our mother had a child every year for six straight years. She took a year off and then had three more children in the next three years or so! Every time Dad walked past one of the bed posts, she would have a child nine months later!

Well, at least that was Dad's humorous way of explaining why we had so many children in our family!

So I was the firstborn female and expected to shoulder much of the family responsibility as a "second-Mom," and it was just not fair. My positioning in the family lineup naturally forced me to take on a very unique role. My nickname spoke volumes……. "Mumsy." Yikes! *Didn't that tell all*?!

I was overprotected "in public" by my older brothers and deemed the "second-Mom" by my very loving sisters. Mom and Dad also came to me as the deciding voice when squabbles and fist-a-cuffs broke out. Just last week, Mom was deciding whether or not to "ground" one of my sisters for a week, and I happened to be in the vicinity when all the commotion went down. I had to weigh in on her banishment to home confinement. Needless to say, my sister was not very happy when I agreed to her grounding!

What was a fifteen-year-old girl to do with such a family? I loved them all so very much, regardless of their unique, extremely persistent, and sometimes "out-of-control" personalities. At times, the pressure of being a responsible young adult at my age was more than I cared to put up with. Yikes!

As a very shy and unassuming female who blushed bright red at the drop of a hat, it pained me greatly when anyone from the opposite sex offered a word or two of exchange. I simply panicked at each and every opportunity of conversation with a boy, and my mind always went completely blank.

I stumbled and bumbled my way through school, painfully mindful of my severe conversational inadequacies. It was embarrassing, to say the least. My extreme self-conscious nature simply swallowed me whole every chance it got.

A handsome neighbor boy noticed I was working in our garden after school the other day and came over to strike up a conversation and offer some assistance. Well, that didn't go so well. I turned three shades of red, mumbled a few words of nonsense under my breath, and went running for the hills (into our house) as fast as I could! He must have thought I was an idiot! So… there it goes!

I suppose the small-town experience and existence in rural Maine churned out many more children just like me. Even with that *tiny bit* of solace and reflection, I was only partially comforted.

School was never something I longed for when fall rolled around but something I simply must put up with because Mom and Dad said I needed a "bit of education" and it would serve me well later on in life.

So I endured these long, hard months of tedious education in my formative years to satisfy their goodly parenting demands, concerns, and advice.

Mom was the fiery personality in the family, of Irish and American Indian descent, who kept everyone on their toes, while Dad was the stoic and sedentary Englishman who didn't have much to say. But for whatever reason, they were a perfect match made in heaven. By the way, when I say fiery, I mean fiery! Look out!

Mom's first name was Catherine, but Dad often referred to her as Katy-girl or Mrs. Clinch, depending on the situation. Mom referred to Dad as Al, honey, or, when she was mad, Albert. Mom had a "practiced knack" at carrying out the name Albert for very long and protracted periods of time when she wanted to get his "undivided attention."

This particular end of school year and the beginning of summer were especially important to our entire family. Dad had recently accepted a new position as a lighthouse keeper off the coast of Friendship, Maine. The lighthouse was located on a tiny exotic island where nature meets its Creator-God, so I was told, or at the very least, self-imagine.

Our parents mentioned it was only the third lighthouse to be built in the entire State of Maine! Dad was the sixteenth man to serve the state in such an honorable and distinct capacity since the early eighteen-hundreds.

Mom and Dad also said it was some sort of "privilege" to have been offered such a position. I must admit I was having a *tad little bit* of trouble wrapping my brain around the "privilege" aspect of our new soon-to-be home out in the middle of who knows where! How would I ever start growing into an intelligent and well-rounded woman with such isolation and dreadful conditions as these?

The announcement of Dad's new job had all nine siblings buzzing with excitement, wonderment, curiosity, sadness, and just a *wee little bit* of caution thrown in too.

All of us kids were running the gamut of emotions in preparation for, and in anticipation of, our new and enchanting Maine island lighthouse dwelling place.

An island home! Franklin Island! Yea! The questions were now starting to pile up and rifle through our minds, trying to fill in the blanks of the now inevitable move.

Friendship, Maine? Where was that? Was it close to Canada? Was Franklin Island next to the shore? Could the ominous and raging seas reach our home? Would we be able to quickly maneuver back and forth to shore as needed? Was it safe? How big was the island, and would our new home accommodate all eleven of us in a comfortable way, or would we be crammed in like a pack of sardines as we were now? Would we have our own bedrooms (fingers crossed)? Where would we go to school? Would we have to go to school (fingers crossed again extra tightly)?

I was so very worried that all of us children would not gain the experiences needed to thrive and prosper later on in life. God uses both experiences and the Bible to help shape and mold us into the image of Christ. I needed a lot of shaping and molding for sure! However, could we count on an island setting to be the remedy for our continued growth? I had many doubts and fears about this!

Well, as an ill-equipped fifteen-year-old girl with few real-life experiences under her belt, one could only imagine the range of questions and anxieties bouncing around my brain right now. The questions were simply endless; however, they would soon be answered in a big, dramatic, and life-changing way.

2

OUR FIRST LEG

ON A BEAUTIFUL FALL DAY IN SEPTEMBER OF 1913, WE SET OUT on our journey to Friendship, Maine, to experience our "privilege" of a new beginning and exciting island experience. Our family prepared all summer long for this long and grueling anticipated journey. We were told that just beyond the hospitable and quaint little town of Friendship, Maine, lay Franklin Island, situated in the treacherous headwaters of Muscongus Bay, which paved the way to the awe-inspiring and majestic Atlantic Ocean. So far so good!

We said our goodbyes to family, friends, our pastor and his wife, and others who had an impact on our lives. We would greatly miss the Goodlander family. Pastor Goodlander could sermonize something fierce, and there was plenty of it too! However, along with his long-winded sermonizing, he had a terrific sense of humor, which I greatly admired.

Much like President Abe Lincoln, whom I read about in the history books, Pastor Goodlander could pop out a funny story or a perfected quip at the drop of a hat to fit any occasion. It was a gift that seemed to come naturally to him and one that kept on giving!

I remembered one funny story he told us about a funeral he was asked to perform.

As he play-acted the story out, he said, "There was a large crowd of about two hundred people who attended a funeral service that I was asked to perform because it was a politician whom the local townspeople liked very much."

"They came from far and wide just to get one last glimpse of old fire-breathing, dead corpse! Halfway through my pious eulogizing, a very serious and determined-lookin' fella raised his hand high with a back-and-forth motion in the middle of the ceremony."

"It took me aback just for a moment, but I thought to myself, *Self, you best try and figure out what this man wants.*"

"So I asked him straight up in the middle of the service, not knowing what to expect, 'Do you have a question or something to add, brother?'"

"With a sheepish little throat-clearing grunt and arm in the air waving back and forth, replaying his initial arm-raising gesture, the man replied, 'No preacher man, I am just swaying holy hands to your professional eulogizing, lifting my holy hands with praise!'"

Pastor Goodlander then looked at us while recalling that story, with his own arms now raised high in the air demonstrably swaying back and forth in an overtly dramatic fashion, and commented, "I could hear the rise of a slow but steady chorus of rapturous giggles and laughter in the church trying to be suppressed for fear of open rebuke and censure for disrupting the seriousness of such an important funeral ceremony!"

Pastor continued, "Evidently, this man had strong attachments to the local Pentecostal Church in the area, which we considered to be fellow brothers and sisters in Christ, but not *quite* our particular stripe! He sure was enthusiastic!"

Once at our own local church in Scarborough, Maine, Pastor Goodlander went on for two whole hours! All I could figure was that he must have had a special unction from the Lord for one reason or another.

I looked over at my father, who had his head tilted back and arms folded in front of him, echoing the rip-roaring sound of thunder through his nostrils and throat. Mom immediately caressed his hand with a soft and gentle touch so as not to make a big scene. She got no response.

She then tugged on his arm and shook him *a tad little bit* harder to force him out of his very deep, tranquil, and restful slumber. This time, her additional slight tug worked like a charm.

Startled, Dad immediately sprang to an upright position with enthusiasm and yelled out in the middle of the Sunday night service, "Amen! Give it to 'em, preacher man, and let them have it with both barrels!"

Pastor Goodlander didn't miss a beat and replied, "I appreciate your very generous contribution to our service, brother Albert!"

Red-faced and completely embarrassed, Dad never again fell asleep in church.

As we said our goodbyes, each of us also made our peace with any misgivings we might have had about Dad's new lighthouse keeper position. We just needed to have faith and trust that everything would work together for good. It couldn't be all that bad, right? The isolation, I mean. I was so excited about our new adventure but very worried about the remote nature of the island.

Fortunately for Mom and Dad, the government official from the U.S. Lighthouse Service who hired my father made provisions to move us to our new island home free of charge. While all the hype about the new automobiles sweeping America had not quite reached rural Maine yet, we were still quite satisfied that a couple of rugged and sturdy horse-drawn covered wagons with all of our scarce earthly belongings would perform the work just fine and get us to Friendship, Maine, without a hitch! From there, we would make a "short" ocean hop to our own personal island getaway, Franklin Island, Maine!

Our family had been working out all the details for the first leg of our journey with much forethought. All of us girls, including Mom, decided to make the journey in one covered wagon, while all the bratty boys, including Dad, got to hang out in the other.

Mom and Dad decided to separate us for fear of having a series of no-holds-barred, knock-down-drag-out fights when we started to

get on one another's nerves. That happened from time to time, especially with the five boys. I thought my parents made a very good call
to separate us for the trip.

*Our covered Conestoga wagons were just what the doctor ordered on our way
to Friendship, Maine. (National Museum of American History)*

The first day of our trip was perfect. There wasn't a cloud in the
sky. The temperature was expected to warm up to seventy degrees
during the day and go down to fifty-two degrees that night. A perfect mix of outstanding weather conditions that allowed for both a
restful night's sleep and traveling mercies during the day.

Everyone seemed to have an extra hop in their step that first
day, Mom and Dad included. The horses also seemed to be full of
vim and vigor as they plodded along with the grace and ease of two
rugged Conestoga horses.

How Dad ever got the U.S. Lighthouse Service to spring for a
couple of Conestoga horses in their prime instead of a couple of old
beat-up mules was well beyond me. *Mind you*, we weren't complaining!

Leaving Scarborough and Portland behind, we were optimistic
about reaching Freeport by mid-afternoon and Brunswick by night-
fall. We wanted to pull a complete ten-hour wagon shift on our first

day of traveling to get ahead of the game, just in case we encountered any bad weather during our three-day land journey. In hindsight, this turned out to be a spectacular move by our rough-and-tumble wagon masters.

I must say I was having a very difficult time understanding the words spoken by our wagon masters. They had some sort of a Down East Maine dialect with a bunch of French thrown in that I couldn't quite get my arms around. I tried to hone in on what they were saying but only picked up every third or fourth word they were muttering! It was all a bunch of *jibber-jabber*! Mom and Dad were doing a little better job of picking up on all of their *mumbo jumbo*!

For the most part, the dirt roads were in fairly good shape on our first day of traveling in our wagons. Every once in a while, we encountered a fallen limb or tree and the occasional wide, obnoxious ruts, grooves, and potholes in the road, but our Conestoga "stallions" were pulling through those just fine.

To cut down on time and miles, our wagon masters decided to hug the coastline on our way to Friendship. They reasoned that the time saved would far outweigh the additional moisture and wetlands we would potentially encounter. Made sense to me, but more importantly, it made sense to Mom and Dad. I respected my parents' judgment.

These wagon masters who were driving our wagons reminded me of the old rough and tumble cowboys we read about in stories about the Wild West. They were blunt; a bit uneducated; spoke and lived like the Down East Mainers we always heard and read about; were experienced in the vast outdoors and rugged terrain of Maine; had a high degree of common sense and intuition; loved to make money ("making them some clams"); and had the intestinal fortitude to get things accomplished, post haste!

They introduced themselves to our family as Hammer and Roy, but they said it as fast as they could (Hammer-Roy) to get a "rise" out of us! A "rise" they did!

As soon as the words Hammer-Roy (hemorrhoid) left their lips, some of our family members let out howls of gut-wrenching laughter. Hammer and Roy joined in the festivities and explained the origin of such a combination of names.

In his broken English, Hammer said, "We were at school tryin' to git us some learnin' in when we got ourselves in a round of fisticuffs with some fearsome lookin' fellas. Bout right when we squared off for a round or two duking it out, they called us some names dat we be two French-Canoocks and look like a couple of 'hemorrhoids.'

"I was pretty quick on dat dere draw and ask em how comes they knew are names? I told 'em dat my name is Hammer and this hea-yah best friend is Roy! They did bust-a-gut laufin and decided to go home. Guess those they-yah names just stuck after a spell!"

We thought we got their story down. As it turned out, they were best friends in high school. One day, they got into some sort of fist-a-cuffs at school with a few class bullies, and in the middle of the squabble, their opponent yelled at them in a fit of anger and said, "You two French Canucks are a couple of "hemorrhoids!" To which one of our now wagon masters replied, "How did you guess? My nickname is Hammer, and this is my best friend, Roy. Together we are known as Hammer-Roy."

Their opponents started laughing uncontrollably, couldn't continue with the fight now that their anger was gone, and decided to go home. The names just stuck after that.

From that day forward, they proudly referred to themselves with such crass, disgusting, and ignorant names. They must be a couple of *ignoramuses*. Only in the State of Maine would someone be proud to take on the names of Hammer and Roy in the aforementioned sense. It did, I suppose, make for an interesting story and a bit of laughter thrown in too!

It might depend on whether such raw name descriptors taken out of context would qualify as humor or not. My brothers certainly liked it! I bet Huckleberry Finn would've liked it too! I saw Mom and Dad with wide grins on their faces as well! You just never know what a couple of Down East Maine *hooligans* would come up with!

I must say I was so impressed with our horses. Outside of a *couple-three* watering holes and rest stops, these Conestoga horses diligently closed the gap between Scarborough and Friendship, Maine, with absolute ease. And the best thing of all was they were as "friendly" as all "giddy-up!"

They were also very patient when all nine of us kids crowded around them, petted them, and tried to feed them things they probably shouldn't be eating. Once we heard that they liked sugar … well, game on!

These horses were very well-known for their strength, muscular build, and docile temperament, which were a perfect mix when pulling wagons and interacting with people. Their basic instinct was to pull lots of weight over long distances in very short periods of time.

Mom also told us they were considered draft horses and were in the same distant family as the Clydesdale horses. They were both believed to have distant breeding genes from the Flemish draft horses in the country of Belgium.

Hammer-Roy (hemorrhoid) in 1913 with some Conestoga horses and a couple of wagons, "making themselves some clams."

Anyhoo, all I knew was that they might not be as stylish, regimented, or as proud-looking as the Clydesdales, but they sure could pull these wagons and were sociable four-legged creatures!

So it was now midafternoon on our first day of travel, and we had reached our first preplanned landing spot in Freeport, Maine. Since we were a little ahead of schedule, my father asked the wagon masters (yes, Hammer-Roy) if it would be alright to stop by the new L.L. Bean Store that had opened up a year ago in 1912 and was all the craze and the talk of Southern Maine!

People everywhere couldn't stop talking about L.L. Bean and their rugged winter clothing line and Bean Boots. As we arrived, Mr. Leon Bean was manning the store. He was a pleasant sort of fellow who seemed to be a man on a mission.

We told him our story about Dad being offered a lighthouse keeper's job working for the State of Maine, living on an island in the middle of nowhere. Mr. Bean proceeded to outfit our entire family with brand-new boots for free!

I couldn't believe it! Get out of town! Seriously?

He said, "If you nice folks are dedicated and foolhardy enough citizens to do that kind of work for the State of Maine, then you all deserve to have dry feet and warm toes! The boots are compliments of the L.L. Bean Company!"

Mom and Dad were so elated and overjoyed that they couldn't stop thanking Mr. Bean enough for his generosity. They were jumping for joy or, at the very least, "jumping for Beans!"

Years later, Mr. Bean's generosity would be repaid many times over by our family in ways you couldn't even imagine.

With joy and appreciation in our hearts, we left Freeport and L.L. Bean that mid-afternoon in the fall of 1913 and headed north-northeast to our first overnight stay in Brunswick, Maine.

We were so infatuated with our new Bean Boots that the wagon ride to Brunswick seemed to fly by in no time at all. We all checked into an old, run-down, crusty, beat-up motel that afforded us a couple of decent-sized rooms to lay down our heads for the night.

This was compliments of the State of Maine. I was beginning to like all of this free stuff just for living on an island. It didn't make any sense to me. At least ... not yet.

With sleepy eyes and cranky dispositions, we were being summoned out of bed at 5:30 a.m. to start getting ready for day number two of our onward march to Franklin Island, Maine.

Yes, that would be 5:30 a.m.! Ouch! I was not an early riser by any stretch of the imagination. I was a *tad bit* grumpy and irritable this early in the morning. Stay out of my way! If anyone decided to speak with me in the morning hours before I'd had a second cup of coffee, I just might bite their heads off! With a few irritable grunts, I gave everyone an early warning signal not to mess with me!

The Clinch family contingent was doing their duty and would be ready to depart at 6 a.m. sharp. I must say each of our wagon masters doubled as taskmasters when it came to being on time. For them, time was money, and they stuck to their schedules and made no bones about letting us know. All these two seemed to want to talk about was "making themselves some clams!"

Day two of our journey was less than idyllic. The temperature very quickly dipped down into the high twenties last night, and at 6 a.m., it was still hovering in the low thirties.

I didn't care what fellow Mainers said about "thick blood;" to me, cold was cold and freezing rain was freezing rain! One could claim all the thick blood they wanted; thirty-degree weather with freezing rain would soak you *down to your gills* and chill you right to your bones *in a jiffy*.

Anyhoo, it was cold, windy, overcast, with some freezing rain thrown in every once in a while, but it didn't seem to bother our sturdy Conestoga horses.

As for the rest of us, however, it had been a very quiet first couple of hours until the cold and occasional freezing rain broke, and I barely heard a peep out of anyone. It was all we could do to stay warm and forget about the blustery cold wind *smacking us upside our heads*. And, yes, we soon began fussing at each other with our childish antics!

It was about 10 a.m., and Mom had just decided it was time to sing a few church hymns to get the blood flowing again and take our minds off the cold weather. She started us off with John Newton's "Amazing Grace" and fully expected every single child to contribute in a loud, vociferous, and engaging way. There was no way out!

Mom knew very well what she was doing! She called out anyone who was not contributing and frequently yelled out the word "louder" to encourage us when we seemed to be trailing off. Even our wagon masters joined in with our out-of-tune sing-along.

I was not quite sure if Hammer-Roy enjoyed participating in the music sing-along or was just a little "a-scared" of Mom and her very firm and direct mannerisms. I guessed it might be a little bit of both!

Whatever the reason, it was nice to see and hear them participate in our singing. Our family always tried to be a good encouragement and influence when opportunities presented themselves.

The singing had been going on for over an hour now, and it was working. We sang all the familiar Christian songs like "How Great Thou Art" and "It is Well with My Soul." We ended with "Rock of Ages," which we thought mightily appropriate to our new, much-anticipated, rugged and rocky coastline that accompanied our island lighthouse home.

At the end of our hymnal hour, we were refocused and reenergized to deal with the remainder of day number two of this bona fide traveling extravaganza! However, some might like to call it a traveling circus. I suppose it depends on one's point of view.

Wiscasset was our next landing spot and overnight accommodation. We arrived about 5 p.m. that evening. It was a small, picturesque little fishing and *lobsta* village, where everyone seemed to be earning a living from the ocean or in some way connected to maritime activities.

Outside of wagons, buggies, and the very rare automobile sightings, the only other way to and from Wiscasset was by train. Well, I suppose the adventurous types could navigate the ocean blue up and down the coast *a piece,* but that wasn't an option for us.

Wiscasset had a train station, a post office, and a general store, which was our second overnight stop. This general store would also serve as our restaurant and sleeping quarters for the night since they rented out vacant rooms located up and over the top of the general store.

This restaurant also had a very small three-table eating area that screamed, "Cockroaches, anyone?" Okay, okay, I knew I needed to behave!

However, we just fell in love with the small-town atmosphere and charm of Wiscasset, Maine. I think it was because we could get out of the Conestoga wagons for a while, get some food, and get some much-needed space. I don't know whether it was freedom or not, but whatever the reason, I could honestly say Wiscasset was a *wicked good* place. Friendly people, great food, and lots of new sights to see!

Mom and Dad gave us leave to go exploring as long as all nine of us stuck together. That was the agreement and promise Big Chief (Teddy-17), Razor (Willie-16), and I (Mumsy-15) had to commit to before all of us kids could go off exploring for an hour or so.

We immediately headed directly down to the Sheepscot River to see what we could get ourselves into there. It was a blast. We collected all kinds of "stuff" that floated to the banks of the Sheepscot. All shapes and sizes of driftwood, weather-polished stones, a couple of water-soaked boots, an old fishing rod, a busted-up old wagon wheel, and whatever else made its way to the banks of that river we checked out and admired.

Of course, Hocker (Peter-13), who was the business mind in the family, wanted to try to sell some of our newly found treasure back to the locals, but the rest of us overruled his untoward business attempt. We just rolled our eyes at him with looks of disgust. However, we did take a few keepsakes with us to remember this town by.

By the way, I must say Hocker had a natural flair for business and selling things. Ever since he was a very young child, he was forever trying to "hock" things for a penny or two.

His selling attempts included everyone in our immediate and extended families, everyone at school, all passersby unawares, and even church folk until Mom and Dad told him to knock it off!

When it came to business, this kid was fearless. He seemed to get an incredible amount of joy from turning a dollar or, at the very least, convincing people of his point of view. It was fascinating to watch his selling skills for such a "young buck!"

The sun was beginning to set, and we needed to head back, post haste. We arrived at the general store around 6:30 p.m., just in time for a proper *lobsta feed*. *Lobsta* was so plentiful in the greater Wiscasset area that it was dirt cheap, and we kids loved every morsel that we were jamming down our throats and bellies right now!

However, I was so very surprised that Madelynn (Mad-14), who was so very prim and proper all the time, could scoff down two whole *lobstas*! I was shocked and taken aback when she asked for that second one!

I didn't believe we would ever let her forget about these two *lobstas* for the rest of her life. With all of Madelynn's pretense and her *high muckety-muck* and prim and proper ways, her façade came tumbling down as soon as we saw the trickles of butter slowly streaming down her cheeks!

She also had a gluttonous look on her face that would not soon be forgotten. A sight for sore eyes and one for the Clinch family memory book for sure! Way too funny!

We ended up climbing into bed around 9 p.m. to be ready for Mom and Dad's 5 a.m. wakeup call. The wagon masters said we should arrive in Friendship around 3 p.m. tomorrow, completing the third and final day of the land portion of our trip. That was very nice to hear. Such a blessing!

Well… best laid plans. We all woke up at around 3 a.m. to the awesome and frightening clap of thunder and flashes of lightning that seemed to shake the entire building.

This was not a very good sign for the roads we were about to travel on. At Mom's direction, we were now praying that the winds and the heavy rains would subside enough to allow us to continue on our way.

Then, all of a sudden, we heard loud, obnoxious, incessant pounding on our bedroom door. Hammer-Roy (hemorrhoid) was knocking on our doors to let us know we were going to delay our departure for just about an hour to see if better conditions might be ahead.

I thought to myself, "Some Christ-like patience will go a long way; everything will be alright."

It was now 7 a.m., and the weather had let up considerably, but it was still pouring a light, steady mist that soaked everything in its path *to the gills* because of the very high winds.

Hammer told us he and Roy had just decided to jump in the wagons and proceed to our next stop in Friendship, Maine. No questions, no looking back!

Hammer stated enthusiastically, "We need to git ourselves down the road a piece wit no fussin' and wishin' backwards."

I thought to myself, "Alrighty then, I gotcha!!"

The slow and steady slog of the Conestoga horses was a pitiful sight indeed. We couldn't believe our eyes at their willingness to continue to pull our wagons without the very slightest touch of a horsewhip or any other kind of inducement, especially with this miserable weather we were having right now. They just instinctively knew they were to pull, and pull they must!

We were now encountering a bit of trouble as we approached the banks of a medium-sized river that had recently overflowed. *Tell a lie*, it was a big problem! Hammer-Roy (hemorrhoid) were none too pleased. I saw it as an opportunity for faith and patience. This wonderful experience was all of God's making, and we needed to live in the moment. *Lord, please help us grow!*

Hammer rattled off a few choice words I cannot repeat with his Down East Maine dialect but otherwise grumbled, "Well, isn't that they-yah just a fittin'. We cahn't git they-yah from hea-yah!"

Roy confirmed the predicament and said, "Ayuh, looks like we got ourselves quite the gullywhumper hea-yah! Going to take some figrin to git round this hea-yah gullywhumpin con-trastophie!"

After jawing back and forth with each other for what seemed like an eternity, Hammer finally muttered, "This hea-yah Roy is tinkin dat we need to be bout attachin' that they-yah gullywomped road up yonder a piece 'bout a hundred fitty foot."

Evidently, if Mom and Dad got this right, Hammer-Roy (hemorrhoid) believed the only option we had was to cut a path around the main road that overflowed and reconnect to it about one hundred and fifty feet further up.

At least that was what Mom and Dad were thinking and hoping they said. Our wagon masters thought they had found a solution to our problem. We'd see!

The boys immediately took out our family's small hand-held axes, and all of us chipped in clearing brush, cutting down saplings, and clearing an alternative pathway around the overflowed river banks. We were completely soaked!

There was just one little unanticipated problem. We didn't realize the underbelly of the area we had just cleared was saturated with water about six inches underneath, and when the first wagon started down our new pathway, it instantly got stuck in the mud. Their solution didn't work, and we were now back at square number one! Not good! It took us about another hour to regroup and get that wagon on dryer ground and pull her out of the "quicksand-like" mud.

Hammer, with a frown on his face, quipped, "This hea-yah is now costin' me some very big clams!"

We now needed to get back to work, cutting a wider swath, swinging around the wet areas, and then reconnecting our second attempt to the main trail again. Outside of a few adjustments, this time it worked like a charm! Many hands make light work! *Thank you, God!*

In total, we lost a little over two hours of travel time, delaying our arrival until 7:30 p.m. that evening. That ain't too bad! I didn't care what Hammer-Roy said!

We arrived in Friendship soaked, exhausted, cold, and ornery. It had been a miserable day, but the worst was now behind us. I was so very thankful to God for the overall safety and comfort this journey had afforded us. His provision and timing were perfect! *Thank you, God, for your exceptional plan.* It was time to get settled in for the night before embarking on our "short" ocean hop to Franklin Island.

The captain and owner of the "auto-boat," who was also our guide, would take us to our final destination tomorrow. Mr. Jedidiah Grassenpoop (pronounced graws-sen-pop) was also the person who would be putting us up for the night. He was a dedicated Quaker whose family came over from England (via Holland) and initially settled in Pennsylvania.

After a few years, his father had a business opportunity that moved their entire family to Massachusetts, where Mr. Grassenpoop primarily grew up. When he retired, he and his wife, Isabella, decided to settle on the rocky coast of Friendship, Maine.

When we arrived at his humble abode, we could not believe our eyes! It was an entire family lodge with twelve bedrooms, two fireplaces, a gigantic kitchen, and beds as soft as feathers. How did people afford this kind of wealth and luxury?

Each of the stately bedrooms had the head of a different alluring and captivating animal that "Mr. Jed" had felled overseas while hunting. As he explained it to us, he would donate the meat from the game to a local tribe or community and then keep the head as a trophy for home.

All I could say was he must be a very good shot since there were heads and horns all over this lodge. I was quite surprised that his wife, Isabella, would put up with all the reminders of the bloodshed and gore on the walls of her very lovely and elegant home. Then again, I often heard the expression that true love conquers all!

Mr. Jed was a wealthy businessman who took over his father's courier business when he prematurely passed away at the age of forty-nine. Having grown up in the Massachusetts courier business at a very early age, Mr. Jed was driven to success.

As he liked to tell the story and reason behind his motivation and drive for success, it all went back to his last name, Grassenpoop. He was unmercifully ridiculed and made fun of by his peers as a child because of his last name.

Mr. Jed mentioned the numerous ways children could manipulate the spelling and pronunciation of Grassenpoop. They were endless. He recalled some of the many variations of his last name with laughter and joy.

However, back then as a child and teenager, the origin of the "I will show them" kind of spirit proved to be beneficial, as it developed an intense competitive spirit within.

He now used his last name as a friendly opening when meeting people and giving folks his calling card for his new auto-boat business.

Mr. Jed cleverly announced, "My name is pronounced Grawssen-pop, without the 'grass' and without the 'poop.'"

It lowered everyone's guard, put a smile on their faces, and put people at ease. This allowed him to start building trust. A very good angle for someone in business.

He sold his courier business in Massachusetts at age fifty-four, moved to Friendship, Maine, and then purchased a very large brand-new "auto-boat" to ferry clients around. It was what he called his semi-retirement business just to stay active.

The new boat would take us back and forth between Friendship and our new Franklin Island home. He had purchased his new Smith and Mabley auto-boat two years ago as soon as the owners, Proctor Smith and Carlton Mabley, started distributing them for sale in the State of Maine.

It was an awesome water *thingamajig,* getting up to 50 mph with good weather and calm seas. Mr. Jed bragged that he could get it up to almost 60 miles per hour, or even a little more if needed, but rarely "stretches her legs" in that way.

We kids were so looking forward to experiencing the power and thrill of this new auto-boat. Each of us had been in a rowboat before but never experienced riding in one with an actual motor! Yippie! I couldn't wait! At least, that's what I thought!

He also bragged that his auto-boat was featured in the 1911 issue of *Rudder Magazine* as one of Maine's early gasoline-powered engines.

Mr. Jed was quoted in the article as saying, "The power boat fever struck me, and it struck me bad, and nothing would help me until I bought a gasoline launch."

In some ways, it reminded me of one of those new automobile *gizmos*, except this machine was on the water and not on roads. The gadgets on the dash looked like an automobile; it had a steering wheel like an automobile; a very loud motor like an automobile; and could go flat out at the drop of a hat! Well, we would see what this new auto-boat was like in the morning!

Mr. Jed's baby—the first Smith & Mabley auto-boat edition in Maine.

Mr. Jed let us sleep in until 7 a.m. the next morning as a result of our disastrous day's journey the day before. We had to be ready to go at 8 a.m. sharp after a large breakfast buffet.

Including our belongings, Mr. Jed estimated it would take four to five trips to get everything to the island. In passing, I overheard him mentioning to Dad that it was approximately six nautical miles offshore to Franklin Island.

Say what? I bout threw a hissy-fit! I immediately ran over to my mother, steaming mad, for clarification on the distance from shore. I was now more worried than ever about the isolation we'd experience! I knew the island was a bit remote, but six nautical miles! Give me a break!

With a very concerned face, I sternly and deliberately asked, "Mom, what in the world are they talking about when they say six nautical miles offshore?"

She told me not to worry and that nautical miles and regular miles were not the same. Okay, that made sense to me ... but what she forgot to tell me, or she didn't actually know, was that nautical miles were LONGER than actual miles!

Come to find out, one nautical mile equals 1.151 of actual miles! Are you kidding me?

Now, this changed everything! I was starting to wonder where we were going and what in the world we were about to get ourselves into.

I mentioned this fact to my brothers, and they just shrugged their shoulders and didn't really seem to care. They were just eager to explore their new Maine island lighthouse paradise!

I was not quite as amenable to the frightful distance from shore. But, then again, what's a fifteen-year-old girl to do other than "jump on board and go with the ocean flow!" While the distance flew in the face of what I was comfortable with because of the apparent isolation, I just needed to trust that God knew exactly what He was doing. It was hard.

It was my very first time on such a boat, and Mr. Jed let all of us kids take a turn steering it on our way out to Franklin Island. He was a kind and fun-loving man in an intense sort of way, if you know what I mean. I suppose he had *a tad little bit* of that Massachusetts edge about him.

The wondering, anticipation, and fret of island living would soon be laid to rest. However, the patience, grace, and Christ-like behavior were just starting to unfold!

3

THE MAIDEN VOYAGE

O N OUR TRIP OVER, THE SEAS IN MUSCONGUS BAY WERE A BIT choppy, and it was quite windy, but the weather certainly could be worse. Mr. Jed's water rig was doing its job, smashing through the waves with precision; however, figuring out how to avoid falling out of the boat and getting wet were our top priorities.

The good news was that the overall weather itself was once again breathtaking. Not a cloud in the sky and already in the mid-seventies, which meant we'd have one of those perfect September days that could only be experienced in the beautiful State of Maine. And, yes, I was partial to my home state. Remember, I was a true-blue born and raised Mainer who made no bones about that fact!

I took it as a blessing from the Lord as He paved the way to our new island home.

However, we still had to contend with those oft and ill-mannered waves. It seemed to me that after every third or fourth "normal" wave, we got hit with a very big, obnoxious monster "fifth wave" that made us hold on for dear life and splashed us right in our faces. It wouldn't take much for someone to flip overboard.

My dad protected folks from the jagged rocky coast and the treacherous headwaters in Muscongus Bay as the lighthouse keeper.

Dad thought the remnants of the prior day's storm impacted the currents.

All of us kids were now getting the hang of it, with a few of us getting seasick during the harrowing ordeal. Not good! Mom and Dad both thought it was a great big joke and couldn't stop laughing. They seemed to be enjoying themselves at our expense.

Well, maybe I am exaggerating again in describing our maiden voyage over, but still, it wasn't all that much fun when everything started spinning topsy-turvy and you wanted to puke!

We needed to remember that accidents can and do happen, and it wouldn't be the first time that an auto-boat capsized.

Yup, you guessed it! Albert Jr (Al-9), JoAnne (Jo-Jo-8), and I (Mumsy-15) were turning three shades of green and letting loose "pukey-pukey" over the side of this *water gismo*. It was our very first time on an auto-boat, and it was getting the best of us.

Mom told us to put our heads down between our knees to help take the seasickness and nausea away. I just couldn't wait to put my feet on solid and dry ground. I loved the "thought" of the new auto-boat experience but was ready for things to get back to normal.

Wait a minute, did I just say back to normal? Who in the world was I trying to kid? Living on an island in the middle of nowhere *all by our lonesome,* six nautical miles offshore, would be anything but normal! I could only pray that the sin sickness of my tormented and faithless mind about our island isolation dilemma was not on par with the intensity of my sea-sick nausea. If so, we were in very big trouble!

Reality started setting in for most of us when we looked back, seeing the mainland fading fast away into something completely unrecognizable. The sight of land becoming nothing more than a disfigured horizontal line on an artist's canvas was a sobering, eye-opening reality check for sure.

Mr. Jed said we were only about three nautical miles out to sea right now. Great timing, Mr. Jed! What else ya got to ease my worries? Please!

It reminded me of that verse in the Bible when Lot's wife looked back when leaving Sodom and Gomorrah and was turned into a pillar of salt. I started to seriously consider the spiritual application to our current situation. I was trying to regain control of my sinful emotions right now!

I could keep on looking back to the comforts of my former life on the mainland, where everything was safe, secure, predictable, and without a care in the world, or I could look straight ahead and embrace God's new chapter in my life and who knew what else! It was the difference between having faith and growing in the Lord or lacking faith and stumbling forward in my own devices!

My deceitful and wicked heart wanted to look back, but my brain wanted to put on the mind of Christ and kept telling me to think about the hope of a brighter tomorrow and look straight ahead. I must admit, I snuck a few peeks from time to time to see just how far we had traveled and what the coastline looked like!

Yikes! Could anyone say wretched seclusion, fear, or how about Swiss Family Robinson? That great novel written by Johann David Weiss back in 1812, where a family got shipwrecked on a remote and uninhabited island, now sounded like it could become our reality! I thought I might change the name to "Clinch Family Survival" or something of the sort!

As we approached Franklin Island, I was starting to get a rush of intense adrenaline. You know that feeling in the pit of your stomach just before you are about to run a race?

Well, I had it times ten. I could tell just by the looks on their faces that everyone else in our family had the same feeling, including Mom and Dad. Yes, there was much excitement and anticipation in the air. Big Chief (Teddy-17), Johnny Boy (Jonathan-10), Reet (Rita-12), and Jo-Jo (JoAnne-8) were beside themselves with excitement and just *a tad bit* over-the-top with their hooting, hollering, yelling, and yipping as we approached Franklin Island.

I was surprised Mom didn't ask them to sit and shut their mouths! I supposed both our parents might be showing an extra measure of grace right now because of the circumstances of our island arrival. We would forgive our obnoxious and hyperactive siblings for now, given the enormity of our last three-and-a-half-day expedition into the great unknown!

As we approached our mooring to tie up the auto-boat and unload our belongings, everyone started pointing to those things on the island that first grabbed their attention and interest.

I was not sure I had ever seen our family more united and cohesive than we were today. We started giving each other hugs, slapping one another's hands with high-fives, and rejoicing at this new island lighthouse adventure. It was as though in an instant, "we became one" in our endeavor of being Maine lighthouse islanders for the good of a holy and righteous cause!

What that cause stood for and was all about would play itself out over the course of the next few years. For now, we just went with "the flow" and soaked up the excitement, camaraderie, the bright, beautiful sun, and the awe-inspiring deep ocean blue.

Our mooring was a "tad little bit" of a hike from the lighthouse, but we didn't mind one iota!

I loved our new home. It looked so very inviting and happy.

Okay, okay, so I was getting a little carried away. But there was a pureness, wholesomeness, and natural beauty in our collective day that couldn't be overlooked and would be talked about frequently over the next fifty years!

And, yes, one hundred years later, it was written about through the eyes of a young woman… Lola is her name. That would be me. I am hoping and praying that hundreds, maybe even thousands, will get to experience what I experienced on that magical, mystical, and heavenly journey when living on Franklin Island. In reality, it was God's plan, and His journey was lived out through His chosen people, the Clinch family.

Our mooring was strategically anchored in the cleft of a solid rock surrounded by the grandeur of God's nature. However, there was a bit of a trick in unloading all of our gear to the shoreline and making sure we didn't lose anything or anyone in the process.

Remember the wind and the "fifth waves" that I mentioned on the way over?

Yup, they were still raging, swelling, and rolling in full force, messing with our unloading process. Timing was everything with these aggravating "Cretan" waves. As soon as the "fifth wave" hit us, we knew we had approximately forty-five seconds to scurry around, unload what we could within that timeframe, and then brace for the onslaught of another fifth wave.

Due to our unloading dilemma, it took us a few minutes to adjust to nature's playpen, but we soon found ourselves artfully navigating the Muscongus Bay tidal currents and wind with only a few exceptions.

Well, we did have a couple of duffel bags go overboard that we quickly retrieved. We lost a few books and some personal belongings, but other than that, we were good. The overboard stuff seemed to bother us girls much more than it bothered the boys. Go figure!

Both the lighthouse and our adjacent home were approximately one hundred yards from the mooring, so we had a bit of a hike. It just didn't matter. We were so hyped-up and full of adrenaline and excitement that making the hundred-yard trek to our new island home seemed like a "fall ocean breeze."

It appeared that each of Mr. Jed's trips would take us about an hour or more as we unloaded and then dragged all of our stuff to their proper destinations, as Mom directed. She was very good at directing and motivating.

I was convinced she should be in the moving and storage business. It would be the most successful moving and storage business in all of America! Mr. Jed even agreed with my assessment. He mentioned that my mom was a great organizer and "director" and could be a very successful businesswoman.

Okay, so Mr. Jed was growing on me despite that Massachusetts thing he had going on. An impediment to his personality to be overlooked since he was such a nice man.

Oh, by the way and for the record, we Mainers had a little angst with our former Massachusetts brothers and sisters. Ever since the divorce from Massachusetts (Maine's Declaration of Statehood), there seemed to be an underlying seed of distrust and confrontation between us!

I'm just sayin'! I knew we'd eventually get through it, but....

4

SETTLING IN AND EXPLORING

AT THE VERY FIRST OPPORTUNITY, THE BOYS SPRINTED AHEAD OF everyone and checked out the specifics of our new home. They couldn't wait to lay claim to a bedroom or two in the hopes that Mom and Dad would say yes.

This house was a very good-sized home by our standards. It had five bedrooms in the main house and a lean-to on the north side, for a total of six. The lean-to was built furthest from the ocean, probably to avoid that wind chill from a cold winter's night or even one of those Nor'easters that we Mainers loved to fantasize and talk about.

I quickly started doing the math in my head about who would end up getting a single room and who would be bunking and doubling up with whom. It would be close, but I just might come away with my own room! Hooray!

I had an ace up my sleeve and might have to do a little negotiating, but I thought I could wiggle myself into my very own *teeny-weeny* bedroom!

Here was how my math played out in the genius inside my mind, or rather, my puny little brain.

Big Chief (Teddy-17) would immediately lay claim to the lean-to so he could have his seventeen-year-old freedom. Mom and Dad would naturally get the biggest bedroom in the house as the master bedroom, so that left four empty, smallish to medium-sized bedrooms for the remaining eight children.

The way I saw things, the remaining four boys would double up in two of the bedrooms, and the remaining four girls would share the other two bedrooms, with the exception of me!

I was laying claim to a little sitting room next to the kitchen, no bigger than an oversized pantry area. It would be a perfect space to call my own. I immediately went to work lobbying Mom and Dad about the need for a fifteen-year-old girl who was coming into womanhood to have her own room!

I sold this idea to Dad first because I knew he would cave to my demands. He then took it to Mom, and with some sweet-smelling words of my own, pleading, a little arm-wrangling, and a few promises, it was a done deal!

Yippee! Lola Clinch (Mumsy-15) had her very own bedroom for the first time ever! I couldn't believe it! I was starting to like this island living thing. Well, at least it was starting to grow on me *a tad little bit*!

Now that we had the bedroom thing under control, it was time to get back to work moving our things from the mooring location to the house. It seemed like it would be an all-day event based on the time it took to unload and carry the first load of our personal belongings.

Mr. Jed was already on his way back to Friendship to pick up another load. He said he planned on using the fourth trip that day to Franklin Island to carry some of the firewood we would need for the winter. He estimated we needed six cords of wood for the winter, but he'd bring seven cords just in case.

Mr. Jed cautioned us, "You just never know when you'll have an extra frigid Maine winter with below-zero temperatures for long stretches of time so far off the coast and *on such an isolated island*. You nice folks need to be prepared to bundle up warm and stoke that simmering red-hot fireplace with lots of wood!"

I mused, *Thanks for the additional reminder of how far away we are from civilization, Mr. Jed! You've done nothing but add to my concern and anxiety about the distance from shore!*

The second load was scheduled to arrive at noon, so we had a little more time to explore. Dad had already beat us to the punch, spying out the lighthouse. This would be his home away from home and constant companion, as his job represented some very big responsibilities.

People's safety and lives were at stake, as Dad helped the ships and other maritime craft navigate the particulars of Muscongus Bay during foggy conditions and other types of inclement weather.

The rocky coast in the bay could be dangerous, and many ships had met their doom as a result. Recently, a five-masted schooner called the Cora Cressey, used for coastal trade and an occasional lobster pound, was caught in a storm and went down and bottomed out!

The Cora Cressey was "swamped" and put down in the ominous and foreboding headwaters of Muscongus Bay!

I soon learned Dad's job was much more than flashing a light on and off. There were log books to keep for the government; cleaning, polishing, and performing maintenance on the lighthouse structure; cleaning and changing the actual lights; and managing supplies and inventory. He was also told that, because of the unique wildlife activity on the island, he would provide tours for sightseers upon request.

Sounded like my father would have his hands full!

At least that's how he made it out to be for Mom and us kids. I guessed he would sneak in a little reading time here and there and still have plenty of time to tinker with all of his metalworking hobbies as well!

The lighthouse was a beautiful structure with a three-foot-wide spiral staircase looping around fifty-seven feet high up in the air. The staircase was a bit tricky since there were no guardrails to hold on to. It was wide open around the edges, and people needed to be very careful. The base was where a majority of the lighthouse supplies were kept, while the middle portion of the structure contained a little office, a sitting area, and a window. At its base, the lighthouse was twelve feet wide, and the parapet at the top tapered up to about eleven feet.

The lighthouse spiral staircase reminded me of my growth journey both as a Christian and as a woman. In a spiritual sense, I felt like I was only just starting my ascent to the top of the parapet! My lack of faith, impatience, and the need to do everything myself seemed to be slowing me down! I also wondered if my walk with the Lord lacked any spiritual guardrails for safety!

I could already tell that Dad was anxious to get that middle portion of the lighthouse into a tiny bona fide office and workspace. I just pictured him sitting in his rocking chair, fixing something, working on a project, or getting a book or two under his belt.

Back home, my father had a variety of jobs, but the one he liked most was the metalworking job he had for over twelve years. He loved trying to fit square metal pegs into round metal holes or some such thing. If metal was involved and something needed to be either made or fixed, Dad was "Johnny-on-the-spot!" He couldn't get enough of that solitary problem-solving metal-type work.

And by the way, he was very good at what he did. We were always amazed at some of the things he brought home from work that he either made or was fixing.

The most intriguing part of our first lighthouse tour and experience was the majestic view. It was stunning, captivating, and hypnotic all at the same time. I couldn't put into words how it felt experiencing the view from fifty-seven feet up in the air, looking out over God's created ocean. It made you realize there must be a Creator-God and a higher power to be able to design such perfection.

Anyone who truly appreciated nature and its design would want to shout "alleluia" from the rooftops or, in our case, from the top of a lighthouse parapet!

Even my brothers, who tried to avoid all emotional, sappy, and thoughtful expressions of praise, for fear of chipping away at their inner manhood, were taken aback by the view. Each, in their own individual ways of expression, said something positive about the view from the top of Franklin Island Lighthouse!

Even non-conversational Razor, who never said a word about anything, said, "Wow, this is wicked good!"

Could it get any better than this?

We had twelve complete acres of happiness to explore in between Mr. Jed's much-needed delivery interruptions. We expected him to be very punctual for his predicted noon landing with the second load of our belongings. We were so eager to continue exploring the rest of the island that we tore through that second load and had it up to the house quicker than you could say "Jack Rabbit."

Mom told us to slow down *a tad little bit* for fear of breaking something or hurting ourselves in the process. Once Mom perfectly placed our household goods, we proceeded to go nuts exploring this pristine, untouched, and adventurous island paradise.

One of the very first things that *hit us on the top of our heads* was the number of birds that inhabited Franklin Island. I had never before experienced so many birds in one place in my entire life. We counted fifteen different types of birds within five minutes of our initial scouting around. There must be hundreds more. The birds "kindly" took the opportunity to "initiate" us into their island club! Yuck!

We spotted osprey, common eiders, various types of herons, a black guillemot, tons of seagulls with various breeding markers, many variations of ducks, and a bunch of other nesting types of birds. We were very careful not to mess with their nesting areas because they were everywhere underfoot.

In addition to all the birds and waterfowl, there were endless amounts of raspberry thickets, blueberry bushes, spruce trees, and what looked like roses covering a goodly portion of the twelve acres. Mom told us it was called Beach Rose. All I knew was that it was a delightful sight!

Of course, the boys were stuffing their faces with the raspberries and blueberries to see who could eat the most. I warned them that they might suffer later on that evening, but they just wouldn't listen.

I told them they might experience some of Montezuma's revenge and to be careful. When they would not listen, I pulled a Pontius Pilate on them and said I "wash my hands" of what might happen to them later on. Boys will be boys!

To that end, I laid claim to complete and total victory in my very clear prognostication and prediction of Montezuma's revenge, as the boys spent the next hour and a half outdoors looking for some privacy areas behind the spruce trees with Scott Tissue in hand!

Oh, by the way, this Scott Tissue stuff that came out this year, in 1913, was really good stuff. Soft as a baby's bum!

In addition to raiding the raspberries and blueberries, the boys were already mapping out and eying another area of the island where they planned to build a "proper fort" among the spruce trees.

They built one back home in Scarborough a couple of years back, and it was quite nice for a primitive looking garrison-like structure. Now that they were older, I expected the *"Franklin Island Fort"* to be a much nicer rendition with all the trimmings.

There was no doubt in my mind that the boys would spend much of the summer months camping out in any fort or shelter we erected. Five boys all alone in a fort on an island in the middle of nowhere, six miles from civilization, was a recipe for disaster! *Just you wait!*

Mr. Jed sounded the foghorn to let us know he was approximately five minutes out with our third load of the day. It was now about 2:30 p.m., midafternoon on our very first day on the island, and I was getting very hungry.

We had been so busy exploring and moving that we lost all sense of time. Mom said she'd fix some Bologna and cheese sandwiches as a snack to "tide" us over until we ate our main supper around 6:30 or 7:00 p.m. She said we were having baked beans and hot dogs for supper, which was a favorite of ours and a well-known Maine specialty!

We generally ate supper at 5 p.m., but because of the move, we were making a few adjustments. Fortunately, our initial supply of food came over on the first load. Mr. Jed said he was happy with the way things were progressing so far and should finish up the last load of the day around 4:30 p.m. or so.

After we strategically placed our third load of goods in the house based on Mom's strict instructions, we were off exploring once again. This time, we circled the entire twelve acres of the rocky shoreline. It was fascinating. There was so much to take in.

We saw everything from seaweed to dead animal carcasses to washed-up driftwood. We even spotted the remains of a seal that had been here for quite some time, based on the awful stench and the skeletal remains.

I found one natural beauty that especially piqued my interest. It was a very small ocean inlet on the south side of Franklin Island. It would have made a perfect second mooring location, except for some very big rocks in the way at the mouth of the inlet.

We girls already had our sights set on the inlet to become our own personal swimming and washing-up area. Depending on the tide, it was a five-foot deep, naturally occurring pool-like body of water about ten feet wide and six feet long. Some of the boys said they already "claimed it" as a fishing hole, but Mom and Dad said everyone could enjoy this little blessing from above.

God had even provided a little swimming pool area in the inlet for us. Could you believe that? I could, after what I had taken in today! God's nature was all over the place and completely saturated and consumed this entire island!

Anyhoo, this was the most fun I'd had in quite some time. I thought Mom and Dad would enjoy the walk around the island as well once they got settled in. There was just so much to enjoy!

Mr. Jed's foghorn blasted out for the final time of the day. We all ran down to meet him at the mooring to start unloading what was left. It was about 4:30 p.m., and it didn't take us long at all to riffle through everything. We finally got the hang of quickly unloading things while managing the pesky ocean waves and tidal currents. We only had a few casualties: the few items that went overboard and the three dishes that got busted up.

All of us kids had such a feeling of intense satisfaction in helping to shoulder some of the workload responsibility for the move. We knew our parents needed the help, and we were happy to pitch in.

It was now time to get washed up and get ready for a traditional Maine baked bean and hot dog supper! I couldn't wait. By the way, the hot dogs were those deep red-stained types, which we Mainers like to call "red snapper hot dogs!" Yum!

Dad said the blessing on our meal, and I sensed he was full of genuine thanks and appreciation to the Lord for our four-day traveling adventure. The dining room was loud that night, but no one seemed to mind. We were immensely enjoying one another's company and rehearsing the events of the last four days, which created quite a buzz in the dining area. We decided to hang around and chat for a few hours, and then we went straight to bed.

Exhaustion set in for our family, and we needed to get some much-needed shut-eye. We each said our prayers and goodnights, and then fell fast asleep to the roar of the waves in the ever-present and ominous Muscongus Bay.

5

OUR NEW HOME

IT FELT SO GOOD TO GET A FEW EXTRA HOURS OF SLEEP! EVERYONE agreed that we would sleep in until 8 o'clock on our first full day on the island. After a very exhausting and emotion-filled day, we had earned the right to some additional rest. We were just plum tuckered out! Our emotions were so hyper revved up yesterday that we kids simply came crashing down overnight.

It reminded me of the waves, which endlessly rolled and built into a highly anticipated crescendo before they came crashing down on our Franklin Island coastline. It seemed like they *smacked me upside my head* that morning!

However, with Mom being Mom, she was up at the crack of dawn reading her Bible, praying, making Dad's coffee, and getting the oatmeal ready for our breakfast. She was an absolute workhorse who never seemed to stop and take time for a break or take time for herself. She was a wonderful mother and was always on the go!

I was so preoccupied yesterday with the move and with exploring the twelve acres of land that outside of the bedroom sweepstakes and a general *look-see*, I barely had time to painstakingly go through the entire house and get a "bird's-eye view" of the premises. The very first thing I noticed on the left side of the main door to the house, adjacent to the front porch, was a framed letter from Dad.

I immediately said to myself, "Hmm, that's unusual!"

Everyone who entered our home would be confronted with the letter since it was directly in front of them. It immediately grabbed my attention because it was not like Dad at all to attempt any kind of home decorating. That was solely and firmly Mom's department.

However, this particular home furnishing was much, much more than an ordinary letter. It was titled. "The Franklin Island Compact" in big black letters.

What in the world could this be, and what was my father up to now? I contemplated.

While Dad might be quiet and reserved, every once in a great while, he would surprise us with his spiritual insights. After reading through the two paragraphs in this neatly handwritten cursive letter, it began to make perfect sense to me.

"The Franklin Island Compact" was a slight variation of the Mayflower Compact, written by our early Pilgrim and Puritan Christian forefathers back in 1620. Dad's own version read as follows:

THE FRANKLIN ISLAND COMPACT:

An agreement between the Clinch family members to honor and serve the Lord while stewarding the Franklin Island lighthouse outpost.

In the name of God, Amen. We whose names are underwritten, the loyal subjects of the State of Maine and these United States of America, do hereby commit our unwavering allegiance to the principles found in the very Word of God and to the advancement of the Christian faith with joy.

With this pledge, we commit to think and act responsibly, loving our coastal neighbors as ourselves, while remembering the grace, ease, and power that was demonstrated by Jesus Christ when he roamed the face of this earth.

Signed,
Albert J. Clinch

"Lowly lighthouse keeper for the glory of God."

My dad made sure there was much Christian influence and American patriotism on Franklin Island from 1913 through 1918. I pray that we helped shape the way for future families on the island and for posterity itself. (Photos to the left of this frame by Jeremy D' Entremont and Bob Trapani, Jr. from top to bottom, respectively)

This was my father's way of letting us kids know who we were as a family and what his expectations would be during our tenure on the island. He asked everyone in our family to pray and decide whether they wanted to sign the pledge. We all eventually joined in and signed the solemn pledge.

My only concern was the length of time it took for Razor to sign the pledge. I sensed a little bit of rebellion in his spirit right now. He was so quiet, like my father, that I never really knew what he was thinking. I just hoped and prayed there was no underlying spiritual issue stopping him from signing the compact. The rest of us kids signed the compact within days of its posting. Not so with Razor!

Normally, Dad safeguarded his personal Christian beliefs between him and the Lord. He was a very private Mainer who didn't feel comfortable forcing his beliefs onto others.

So it absolutely did capture our attention and curiosity when we read that compact. It was Dad's own unique and small way of being a testimony for the Lord and telling any visitors who entered our home what to expect. I thought it was a great testimony without forcing our religion down anyone's throat.

If visitors were interested and had questions about the Compact, they could ask, but if it didn't prick their consciences, interests, or spirits, then they could read it and remain silent. At least, that was how I rationalized it inside my mind!

However, on the other hand, the Bible did say, "*The Word of God is quick, and powerful, and sharper than any two-edged sword, piercing even to the dividing asunder of soul and spirit, and of the joints and marrow, and is a discerner of the thoughts and intents of the heart.*"

So I supposed their consciences would be pricked one way or the other by my father mentioning some of the subtle particulars from the Bible in the Compact. Huh!

The house was fairly massive in comparison to what we were used to. Mom and Dad's bedroom was a very good-sized room, and all the kids' rooms were smallish to medium-sized, but efficient.

All the bedrooms had small closets and bureaus enough to stuff our underwear, socks, and other personal belongings in. There was no question that the sleeping arrangements were a little tight, but compared to what we had back on the mainland in Scarborough, it was a definite upgrade.

While there had been consternation, anxiety, and some serious arm wrestling about who would get which bedrooms, the real winners in the bedroom sweepstakes were Teddy and me. Well, I suppose, Reet too, since she rode my coattails to a single room of her own!

Willie (Razor) was having some major heartburn right now about young Reet, who was only twelve, getting her own bedroom while he had to share a room with one of his brothers.

Razor angrily stated, "As a seventeen-year-old man, I deserve a room to myself!

That was where I (Mumsy) had to step in and calm the situation down *a tad little bit*. I took Razor aside and walked him through how the rooms were figured out in a calm and mature manner. He still wasn't buying it. Razor was hopping mad right now.

I said, "How about we make a deal? In a three-month timeframe, if you are still dissatisfied with the sleeping arrangements, I'll give you my room for the next six months, and we can continue to switch on and off. Does that sound fair to you?"

After a few more weeks of pouting, Razor finally relented a bit and said, "Thanks for your offer and for being willing to help out, Sis. We'll see."

Teddy's (Big-Chief) lean-to was structurally secluded from the rest of the house. It was only about six feet wide and twelve feet long. The dimensions of the room were a little awkward, and the room itself was in a state of disrepair for now, but it would do just fine for Teddy. The great thing about his lean-to was that it followed the roofline off the back of the house. It had created a sort of mini mezzanine area to store a bunch of things up and over the top of his room.

My single bedroom was very tiny, but it was mine, all mine, and I loved it! Our great big kitchen acted as a combination dining room and kitchen area, which was quite normal and understandable for our style of house. The room I called the "fireplace room" was cozy and inviting.

Dad had already cranked up the fireplace this morning as a result of the cooler temperatures last night. He had that fireplace roaring, crackling, hissing, and making all kinds of other comforting wood-burning sounds. Sitting by an open fire felt so warm and cozy.

We had running water piped into a couple of areas in the house from an underground aquifer, a tub that needed to be topped off with hot water by hand before each bath, and a small toilet inside. There was also a small outhouse adjacent to the lean-to for convenience when we were outside playing and horsing around and didn't want to traipse mud through the entire house with our dirty shoes. With eleven family members, having a second bathroom was a definite plus, even if it was just a very small privy.

Mom assigned a day and a specific timeframe when each of us would take our weekly baths. She had to boil a goodly amount of hot water over the fireplace in a big metal water-pitcher *thingamajig* just before our scheduled baths. There was plenty of privacy, but things just had to be organized and managed on time for things to work with eleven people.

We did have one mishap when Mom thought the water she was heating up over the fireplace was finished. She brought the pitcher in and left it on the table before Albert started taking his bath. All of a sudden, we heard this loud, murderous screech coming from the bathroom. Mom quickly ran to the door and asked if everything was okay. Come to find out the water was ice cold, and Al was just letting the family know he wasn't a happy camper! Oops!

Outside of our scheduled bath time, we always had the option of grabbing our swimming trunks or a pair of shorts and jumping into our inlet swimming pool in Muscongus Bay. That option would be used quite frequently in the summer months, to be sure, but on rare occasions once winter set in.

Although there had been a time or two back in Scarborough when the boys decided to take the "deep freeze" challenge from our dad in a local pond when they were horsing around and being silly!

One of the other conveniences my father loved about our new home was the hallway connected to the lighthouse. He didn't have to go outdoors to get inside the lighthouse. Such a blessing during rainy days or when any Nor'easter might happen in our direction. There was also a very big screened-in front porch with rocking chairs for those who wanted to sit outside, away from the demon-bugs.

As far as any basement was concerned, we got short-changed in that department as a result of all the ledges on the island. The government decided to put this lighthouse home on a slab with a somewhat small, elevated, and very limited crawl space.

I especially liked the dormers on each side of the house. They would be great spots to curl up with a book on a cold winter's night or when you just wanted to get away from all the noise emanating from our eleven "energized" family members.

These dormers were also terrific lookout spots over the ocean since they provided a complete panoramic view of Muscongus Bay, with the exception of a few *tiny-weeny* blind spots.

My father was also given a heads-up by the U.S. Lighthouse Service that they were working on plans to build a medium-sized one-room auxiliary building on the property to act as a combination function room and museum-like area within a two-year timeframe.

That meant that in a few years, we might have some company for several months on the island while it was under construction. That would be interesting.

When I looked at our new home from a distance, something about its positioning and the way it was located on the property gave it a proud, stately, and almost inviting appearance when approaching the island from the bay.

However, during severe and violent thunder and lightning storms when the swelling seas crashed down and overflowed small portions of our island, the contrast might not be quite as inviting!

I supposed there might be a spiritual lesson woven in with the difference between the two!

All in all, we had a glorious home that couldn't be any nicer. I was so thankful to God for our home, plenty of great food, a toasty fireplace, our health, a wonderful, loving family, and most important of all, my personal relationship with Jesus Christ, our Lord and Savior.

6

OFF TO THE RACES

A S YOU CAN IMAGINE, EDUCATION WAS PRIORITY NUMBER ONE Monday through Friday; Saturdays were an all-out free-for-all with exploring, some chores for Mom and Dad, and then getting ourselves into things we probably shouldn't; while Sundays primarily became our day of rest and worship with a few smallish catch-up items on the agenda *thrown in for good measure.*

By the way, when we turned twelve, on Sundays each one of us was expected to get into the rotation for giving a brief "sermon" on how the Lord had blessed us in the previous week, just before my father gave us the main Bible challenge. It made for some interesting and humorous stories of "blessing."

Recently, nine-year-old Albert (Al – 9), a.k.a. "smarty-pants," gave us one of the best recounts of a blessing for the week that we had heard in a very long time when he mentioned the use of our two toilets.

With a serious look and unflinching matter-of-fact tone, Albert stated, "I'm so thankful that when I have to go pee, I don't have to go outside to use the outhouse but can use our inside toilet instead."

It got the whole family giggling and howling with laughter. Mom and Dad had a rule about not laughing at the "blessing of the week," but we couldn't help ourselves! Mom and Dad had to let this one go because after a few irrepressible giggles themselves, they were also belly-laughing along with the rest of us!

But it got even better. Al wasn't finished with his unknowing, unwitting, and simply hilarious punchline!

Al was *as serious as all git-out* and continued, "Except when one of the girls gets in the bathroom before I do and hogs the entire room for hours when they try painting on their new eyes, lips, and faces."

The boys went absolutely bat-crazy, beside themselves with laughter. The whole family erupted with glee. Out of the mouth of babes!

Mom routinely assigned all nine children their homework for the day and expected strict compliance. We were not allowed to go outside until our studies were finished for the day. That was Mom's secret weapon. No learning, no fun… it was that simple.

This homeschooling thing had been interesting. Mom gave us our assignments and left us alone to get our homework completed. I think it forced me to think on my own and made me a better student. I was still getting adjusted to it, but I thought it might be growing on me. I guessed I would know better when the test grades came out!

Now, there was also a downside. I had to look at the same eight faces day in and day out, and from time to time, we got on each other's nerves. But outside of the "close-quarter combat" that reared its ugly head every once in a great while, most of us were learning a great deal and progressing in our studies.

My parents tried to make school fun at the same time. We took field trips around the island; performed geology tests on the soil and rocks; identified all the various kinds of animals and bugs on the island; grew vegetables in a small garden; made art projects from the driftwood and from whatever else might end up on the rocky shoreline; and performed our physical education classes outside.

For me, the field trips were the best because Dad joined in with talks about the island from his perspective. It was always a treat for our entire family when he actually talked and participated. He was a man of very few words. My father was a loving and concerned parent, but quiet and ultra-reserved.

Sometimes I wondered if Dad's quiet and reserved nature was partly related to Mom's super-charged personality, and he thought it was best to stay on the sidelines and let her take the lead. Regardless, when he told us his stories and thoughts on our field trips, he thoroughly captured everyone's undivided attention.

Speaking of education, I must say a word or two about my brother Albert (Al-9). He was an absolute smarty pants! I had never been around someone so young but so intelligent and accomplished. He was so very special and one of a kind. Mom had all she could do to keep up with his abilities and keep him challenged with school-work. He actually liked this stuff!

Al was far advanced for his age with his reading, writing, science, and arithmetic skills. Almost every week, he surprised us kids with a new *whatchamacallit* invention or something way out of the box for a child his age. He recently made this incredible mallet-like weapon fashioned with stones at the end and a wooden handle that looked like something you might find in Germania back in AD 166! The wooden handle was very neatly carved with leather strips securing the stones and the handle at the end. He was only nine!

I expected big things from Albert when he grew up. I knew there were never any sure things in life and that I shouldn't get too far out in front of my oars, but Al was the real deal and, for my dollar, a sure bet! Well, I didn't bet or anything like that, but you get what I am saying.

The rest of us simply did what we had to do to get by with our studies to keep Mom happy. Beyond our studies, each of us had assigned chores and other projects that popped up now and then at Mom and Dad's request.

Thanksgiving was now weeks away, and Christmas was right around the corner. I was looking forward to each of those holidays this year. This would be our very first holiday season on Franklin Island. We were gaining some ground, getting ready for the long winter season. Not there yet, but gaining.

Firewood was mostly put up, fall cleaning was almost done, weatherproofing our new home was just about finished, the painting was complete, sand for the walkways was piled sky-high, and all that was now left was to get ready for Thanksgiving and some

Christmas gifts for the family. Because there were so many of us, we put our names in a hat and drew names for Christmas. It simplified things a *tad little bit*.

I planned on knitting something for the gifts I intended to give. I loved knitting. It was a little bit of an obsession with me now. I had never really liked crocheting or fallen in love with other kinds of arts and crafts. I didn't dislike them, but there was something about knitting that I couldn't get enough of. I could sit for hours on end and knit. It allowed me to be alone with the Lord.

All of my sisters and brothers had been the current appreciative beneficiaries of my knitting "addiction" these many years. They always looked forward to what "Mumsy" was going to make for them this time of year.

I didn't exactly follow the drawing names out of the hat routine like everyone else because I loved knitting things for everyone! Of course, it was quite an ordeal to keep my gifts hidden in strategic locations so the kids didn't spy them out before Christmas.

I was pretty good now at concealing them, and it drove the boys crazy-nuts not knowing where they were. I thought that might be one of the most enjoyable parts of Christmas for me: hiding my presents from the boys and watching them squirm!

It was the second week of November in 1913, and we were headed to Friendship, Maine. This month, as part of the arrangement Mr. Jed had with the U.S. Lighthouse Service, he provided a quarterly ride to the mainland for our family. We also got twenty-eight days of vacation sometime this year to the mainland, which had to be coordinated with the U.S. Lighthouse Service.

They scheduled an "ocean-floater" to come out and man the lighthouse in our absence for those vacation slots to keep everyone safe on Muscongus Bay. I think the quarterly trip to shore and the vacation time were a result of not wanting their lighthouse keepers and their families to burn out, go stir crazy, get cabin fever, and leave.

Dad told our family it had happened to the last lighthouse keeper on Franklin Island before we took over the helm.

Mr. Almond Twitchell and his wife had only been on the island for two years (1911–1913) before they asked to be reassigned. Rumor had it that Mrs. Twitchell was not happy living that far off the mainland. She gave her husband an ultimatum that they had to get off Franklin Island or else. She was being very "twitchy" about things!

Dad wasn't quite sure what the "or else" actually meant but said it was pretty serious and caused a lot of marital tension between them. The reassignment for the Twitchell's created quite a stir at the lighthouse agency too since Mr. Twitchell was a U.S. Lighthouse Service "lifer" and had a string of solid and successful assignments.

I must admit that being six nautical miles from shore did cross my mind from time to time, and it gave me the *heebie-jeebies*! I was still very anxious about the distance.

While in Friendship for the day, the girls planned to do a little window shopping; go to a local restaurant for lunch; get caught up on any supplies we might need; grab a few Christmas presents and yarn; and see if we could find a few good novels at the local used bookstore. I believed this might turn out to be one of the favorite days of the year for both Madelynn (Mad-14) and Rita (Reet-12) as well.

They were both so caught up with clothes and what the new fashions of the day were that it was sickening. It was clothes, clothes, and more clothes with those two. I must admit it fit Mad's personality to a tee, as she tended to be a little high-minded and *hoity-toity* (some use the term stuck-up), but I was the most surprised by Reet with all her talk about clothes and fashion. I hoped it was just a passing fad for Reet because it didn't fit her sweet little personality at all.

For me, I couldn't care less. I was happy with a baggy pair of pants, some old farm trousers that fit and a jersey, or some hand-me-downs from our extended family. Honestly, I would rather be knitting!

I simply relished the thought of sitting down by the open fire on a cold winter's night, ragamuffin style, knitting away to my heart's delight!

The boys weren't having any part of the "girls' day out" stuff. They said they would meet us for lunch at the local restaurant, but they had different plans. I guessed they'd spend much of their day hanging around the Friendship Trading Post checking out the fishing rods, rifles, ammunition, pistols, and anything else that kills things or goes… "bang!"

Or, perhaps, taking a *gallivant* over to the neighboring towns to *strut like a peacock* in front of the female persuasion!

I also heard they wanted to check out a brand-new Model T down near the Sheriff's Office. The Model T Ford automobiles had been out for five years now (since 1908), and they were slowly making their way into many of the rural areas of Maine.

So far, only the very wealthy could afford them, but they were an exciting new *contraption* that had everyone's interest, including my own. They said the automobile would be a game-changer. Not quite sure what that meant, but it sounded good to me!

Thinking back, I remember Hammer-Roy being a little concerned about the "new mobiles" as they called them. Hmmm …

Anyhoo, the Clinch men, with the exception of Albert, loved what they had been hearing about automobiles and wanted to go down and check it out for themselves. All Albert (Al-9) cared about was his books and would rather be at the used book store with the girls instead of gawking at things he had no interest in.

Willie (Razor-16), on the other hand, loved automobiles but was truly obsessed with fishing and hunting. It all started when he was back home in Scarborough, and Dad would take him, Peter (Hocker-13), Jonathan (Johnny Boy-10), and Teddy (Big Chief-17) fishing and hunting down at the Scarborough Marshlands. Razor was forever bringing home striped bass, large-mouth bass, smelt, sea-run brook trout, and those nasty-looking eels.

So all the boys headed down to the Sheriff's Office *as giddy as could be* about the Model T! The two older boys were so excited that they sprinted the last two hundred feet to take it all in.

In a state of wild imaginative exhilaration, Teddy asked, "Dad, when can we buy one?"

Dad responded in jest, "I promise you boys one thing, sometime before I pass away, I will definitely purchase a Model T! I just need to save up for the next ten or twenty years!"

Each of the boys started cracking up and laughing out loud. They understood that being a lighthouse keeper put the kibosh on anything the least little bit extravagant.

They each took turns sitting in the car and admiring the engine, with a promise to purchase one as soon as they could.

Dad just sat back and smiled as they hopefully proclaimed their desires to purchase a brand-new Model T!

Dad and the boys also started their waterfowl hunting excursions down at the Marshlands but soon graduated a little further inland to the Saco River Basin that included Steep Falls and Limington, where there was some very big game, so they bragged.

As I thought, we had a fabulous time with our one-day getaway from Franklin Island, flitting freely about with not a care in the world. There was just so much to cram into an eight-hour day, and we took full advantage of our limited time.

After our shopping whirlwind (mainly window-shopping), we met Mr. Jed and the boys about 4:30 p.m. at the Friendship Community Boat Launch and were promptly ushered safely back home to our beautiful island lighthouse home.

However, I was often reminded that along with the fantastical beauty of island living came the dreadful loneliness, seclusion, and isolation. I was praying that someday and somehow, we could have our cake and eat it too! I prayed it was possible to live on the island but enjoy the creature comforts of interacting with the civilized world upon occasion. Dear Lord, was that asking too much?

7

HOLIDAY JOY

THANKSGIVING WAS THE TIME OF YEAR WHEN MOM AND THE girls shined the brightest in the eyes of the male delegation in our family. I knew Dad and the boys loved us unconditionally year-round, but the old saying, "The way to a man's heart is through his stomach," applied each and every Thanksgiving time of year.

My brothers just seemed to appreciate us more during the holiday season and go out of their way to be kinder, gentler, and a little less "hostile." Not hostile in the sense of an arch-enemy or anything like that, but hostile in the typical brother-sister relationship kind of way.

I suppose that if I am being completely honest, feeding them lots of great food and giving them lots of presents took the edge off the sibling rivalry for a few months. Whatever the motive, it was a welcome break and relief.

Mom outdid herself that Thanksgiving with an absolute heroic effort! She cooked up a royal feast normally reserved for kings, queens, the wealthy, and the incorrigible elite.

Not so for this particular Thanksgiving Day! On this remarkable day at the island lighthouse paradise on Franklin Island, Maine, it was now our mother's turn to feed the lowly but lovable Clinch gang, not the rich and the famous!

Mom spent countless hours and days in the kitchen preparing enormous amounts of food. It was a complete and total labor of love. There was much more food than our normal Thanksgiving because I think she was trying to make our first Thanksgiving on the island an extra special and memorable one. The girls helped out the best we could, but the main workload was squarely on Mom's shoulders and was all her doing.

That sweet smell of cookies, cakes, and pies cooking on the open fire was very tantalizing to the senses. The aroma filled the house for days. That hot apple cider didn't smell too bad either.

On Thanksgiving day, when my father and the boys came in about 1 p.m. from hunting waterfowl, all we heard from them was "wow" or "incredible" or "awesome" or *looky here!*" They showed a great deal of appreciation for Mom's efforts. Her culinary feast was simply quite a display of grandeur and genius.

Mom was trying to lighten the current moment of praise by performing a little curtsy like a stage actor would at the end of a Shakespearean play. Her little offering of recognition was so cute from a woman who had had nine children and was starting to fill out just a *teeny-weeny* little bit (some use the phrase "a tinsel"). We loved her so very much!

We took full advantage of our island surroundings that Thanksgiving Day. Dad and the boys were shooting up the waterfowl like gangbusters, so we had plenty of meat on the table.

In our case, the "gang" was the endless supply of dive-bombing waterfowl, and the "busters" were the boys trying to thin out the flock a little and rendering a little payback for nailing us with their white and brown excrement each and every day. When the poop got in our hair, it was absolutely nasty and stank!

However, we were so blessed to have a variety of waterfowl on the island for some of our tasty and savory meals. We had common elders, the American black duck, the wood duck, Northern pintail, Northern shoveler, mallard ducks, and various teal species. We not only had an island lighthouse paradise on Franklin Island, but we also had a hunter's paradise too! Very rarely did one of the older boys or my dad ever come home empty-handed.

However, Dad did prefer to oversee and monitor the hunting activity on the island with close scrutiny, probably at the urging of our mother. It all started when Teddy and Willie went off hunting one morning on the back side of the island.

From about eight o'clock in the morning until nine, the two older boys were shooting up a storm. It sounded like nonstop rapid gunfire that morning, and it started to concern our parents. Dad decided to make a quick little visit and wander down to where the boys were hunting. To put it mildly, he didn't like what he was seeing.

As he approached the two boys' hunting spot about fifty feet away, Razor wheeled around in Dad's direction and unleashed a round of shots at a few of the birds in the sky. Dad dove for ground cover, worried he might be shot!

Dad cried out in a passionate voice and asked, "What are you doing? What are you shooting at? Are you trying to get someone killed?"

Razor, now slouched over with his tail between his legs, said, "Dad, I am so sorry for not paying more attention."

Teddy added, "We were so caught up with shooting down the birds that we forgot our hunter safety manners. It won't happen again."

Dad, still in shock and extremely angry and agitated, said, "No, you are correct, it will never happen again!"

From that day forward, Dad made a list of six rules. First, there was no shooting before 7 a.m., just in case people were still sleeping. Second, they could only shoot the number of birds needed for that night's dinner. Third, the waterfowl had to be the proper age, size, and girth for harvesting. Fourth, the boys could only shoot away from the island and not toward the island, for obvious reasons. Fifth, they had to be very cautious that no watercraft *gizmos* of any kind were in the area as far as the eyes and the binoculars could see. Sixth, there was no hunting on Sundays.

"Once these boxes are checked, it is 'fair game!' Understood?"

Besides loading us up with waterfowl, Razor also chipped in with the usual handsome supply of his "catch of the day" from the ocean. The girls also helped out by putting to use the delicious sweet raspberries and the scrumptious blueberries we had picked and canned a few months back when we first arrived on the island. We kept those down in our root cellar with the rest of our vegetables, canned goods, cured meats, cider, dairy products, and other beverages. A good root cellar was a modern-day necessity.

However, I must *fess up* about our raspberry and blueberry picking debacle a few months back! It was a nightmare! All of us girls, Mom excluded, decided that we wanted to pick all the berries Mom would need in November for our Thanksgiving Day dinner. We started picking around 10:00 a.m. and had about two-thirds of the berries we would need. So far so good!

Then the boys showed up around 11:30 a.m. and started pestering us to no end with this and that and were trying to be an overall nuisance to our berry picking efforts. That was when everything started to "fly south!"

With a stern and unwavering voice, I barked, "*Looky here*, if you five boys don't knock it off right now, I am going to whip you with one of these raspberry shoots and give you all a good licking, and you know I will do it too!"

They smirked, chuckled, didn't stop, and their antics grew steadily worse. So I took two steps out into the middle of the raspberry thicket and was aiming to grab the biggest shoot I could find to let the boys know I was serious and wasn't messing around!

Well, that didn't go so well. Oops! I stepped into the middle of a ginormous hornet's nest, and all mayhem broke loose. There were hornets everywhere! The boys took off running for the hills (our house), and we girls grabbed our buckets and tried to keep up. The boys were sprinting full speed ahead, and all we could do was fast-walk so we wouldn't lose any of our freshly picked berries.

They won and we lost. Each of the girls got stung a bunch of times. When I say a bunch of times, I mean a bunch of times! I was *madder than a wet hen* right now! I could count at least a dozen hornet stings all over my body. The worst sting was on the side of my neck. That one got me howling like a mad wolf!

No, I take that back! *Tell a lie!* The worst sting came when we got back to the house and all five boys were there to greet us on the front porch, laughing us to scorn and mocking us!

With fire in my eyes, I asked, "Are you sure you boys want to go there?"

That seemed to put an end to their mockery. They knew "Mumsy" was furious!

Dad continued an important family tradition by saying a beautiful Thanksgiving Day prayer. He thanked God for the blessing of the day and for His goodness, mercy, and grace. After his thoughtful and heartfelt prayer, it was off to the races!

Ladies and gentlemen ... on your marks, get set, go!

Yes, the eleven participants in this Thanksgiving Day race were relishing in this superb culinary feast and delight! Plates and silverware were clanking, voices shouting to pass the particulars, and overall pandemonium ensued for the next one-half hour or so.

One particular moment stole my full attention. After Big Chief loaded up his plate with turkey, stuffing, potatoes, and gravy on top, he closed his eyes, sat back *a tad little bit*, and very slowly put the food in his mouth in a show of pure ecstasy! The entire family took notice and started pointing at Big Chief's dining spectacle! We roared with amusement! I hate to say it, but Big Chief weighed over 260 pounds for a reason! He sure enjoyed his food!

After indulging in the feast, we were so completely stuffed that we asked Mom if we could have our dessert later on in the afternoon.

Can you believe those words had passed my lips? Dessert later on?

She completely understood but jokingly replied, "Why, you don't like my pies, cakes, cookies, and jams?"

Then we received that Mom wink and a smile, so we knew we were temporarily off the hook until our food settled.

After we gorged ourselves *full to the brim* with an unforgettable and delectable feast, everyone stretched out around the fireplace, listening to Mom and Dad take turns reading portions of Louisa May

Alcott's *An Old-Fashioned Thanksgiving*, published more than three decades ago, back in 1882.

Louisa May Alcott was my favorite author from nearby New Hampshire, and our entire family adored her writing!

Then, almost in unison, the boys started hamming it up while Mom and Dad were reading. They were "trying" to playact each section of *An Old-Fashioned Thanksgiving* while it was being read. It surprised me a little, but they weren't all that bad at playacting, even though I gave them a terrible hard time, like any sister would.

I suppose that with a good book, a full stomach, content hearts, while listening to a world-famous author, anything was possible, and the boys didn't disappoint.

Then Mom yelled, "Cleanup time," because it was now time for Thanksgiving Day cleanup duty. This was usually the time when my father and the boys disappeared and became willingly invisible.

Yup, as soon as Mom yelled, they were right on cue and out the door! All of a sudden, the boys in the family had to go take care of some firewood or *some such nonsense.* They hated standing around the kitchen washing dishes, taking care of leftovers, and cleaning up!

No worries, I was not too keen on cutting, splitting, and carrying firewood, so I guessed that made us even. I planned on reminding them of that fact the next time they barked orders to help carry in the firewood!

With Christmas now just two and a half weeks out, we expected one more trip from Mr. Jed to the island before the New Year began. His upcoming trip to Franklin Island was much needed this week so we could build back up our food supplies. With all the holiday cooking Mom was doing these last four weeks, we were getting very low on everything.

It made me realize *once again* just how reliant we were on Mr. Jed for our welfare and physical well-being. Without him auto-boating his way out six nautical miles into the fearsome Muscongus Bay tidal currents once a month, we would be "up the proverbial ocean without a paddle."

That scared me a little bit, and I had been praying about it. *Tell a lie*, that scared me a lot! But, then again, in the end, I had to fully acknowledge that God had the ultimate watch-care over us.

Tuesday of that week was Mr. Jed's landing day, and we were looking forward to some good conversation with someone other than family members. Mr. Jed was always good for a story or two, some updates on local and world news, and a long line of jokes! He was a hoot!

He didn't disappoint us this time either. He rattled off a litany of various things about this and that to the delight of Mom and Dad and us kids. He also brought with him a stack of old newspapers for us to peruse. The kids took in as much as we could but couldn't exactly follow everything he was talking about as a result of that very thick Massachusetts brogue, with a little Quaker *thrown in there too for good measure.*

However, we did hear something that appeared very concerning to our parents and startled us just *a tad little bit.*

Mr. Jed said, "There are rumblings of major military and political conflicts around the world that seem to be growing stronger by the day.

For some reason, Austria, Serbia, Hungary, Germany, and the Ottoman Empire all had angst, hatred, and rivalries with one another, and there is a growing concern that war might break out all around the world."

In my innocence, I responded, "They seem to be all in *such a tizzy*. Someone needs to *knock them upside their heads*."

Mom responded, "Lola, in this case, you might be exactly right. Knocking some common sense into those political leaders might be just what the doctor ordered!"

Dad added, "It all boils down to some common threads. The Bible tells us that the lust of the flesh, the lust of the eyes, and the pride of life were often the genesis of such conflicts. Greed, self-interest, and power drive most of these world leaders."

I then concluded the talk about war, "I don't suppose any of this would make its way to Franklin Island, but it is intensely worrisome to hear about nonetheless!"

 Mr. Jed also said something about a great big canal somewhere near Central America that was about to be finished. That one didn't register with me.

Then he gave us an update on the aftermath of the Titanic sinking last year (1912) and what they had found out about that devastating catastrophe.

Mr. Jed's last volley of news for the day was some very boring news about banking, and that a Federal Reserve System would now be taking over all the money in our country. He didn't sound too enthusiastic on this front.

It was all French to me! I'd let all the *high muckety-mucks* worry about that sort of nonsense.

Just before his departure, Mr. Jed asked if he could speak with Dad alone just for a minute. We all headed inside the house so Dad and Mr. Jed could talk in private. It struck me as a bit odd, but I assumed it had something to do with the U.S. Lighthouse Service.

Whatever it was, the conversation between them only lasted for another ten to fifteen minutes, as Dad came inside the house shortly thereafter.

However, I did wonder why in the world my father decided to come through the lighthouse entrance to our home instead of the front door, since it was closest to the mooring. I wondered what Dad and Mr. Jed were up to, if anything at all?

Tomorrow was Christmas Day, and there was excitement in the air. I had all of my knitting completed and was anxious for Christmas to get here. The names were drawn out of the hat weeks ago, and everyone was secretly tiptoeing and maneuvering around, getting their Christmas presents ready.

Yes, the boys were pestering me like there was no tomorrow and trying to find out where my presents were hidden, but I didn't flinch one single bit. I must admit they got very creative and manipulative with their attempts at finding out where I hid them. They even tried bribing me, to no avail!

God blessed us with a wonderful tree-cutting outing a few weeks back when the snow began to fall as we dragged our tree back home. We ended up getting about six inches of snow in total that day. Since then, two additional snowstorms added another foot and a half to the total snow accumulation.

With the snow now completely covering the roof of the house, the surrounding acreage, and the ocean as a backdrop, it didn't get any more picturesque than this. It was absolutely stunning!

Madelynn (Mad), who was the artist in the family, had been working hard at capturing our very first "white Christmas" on Franklin Island on canvas! She told me not to tell anyone, but she was painting a landscape portrait as a family present for Christmas Day. I had seen glimpses of her initial work when she let me sneak a peek, and it would be a family treasure and heirloom for sure!

Along with our bountiful Thanksgiving Day feast, our tree-cutting adventure would be another special moment for the Clinch Family memory book.

Thank you, dear God, for your love, kindness, and generosity, and for the memories that will last for generations!

The Clinch family presents were stacked *fifty-seven feet high* underneath our big, beautiful spruce tree, which we had cut down as a family. The spruce trees on our island were a combination of native trees and those planted each year by the U.S. Lighthouse Service and were homegrown. A few Northern pine trees were mixed in as well.

The Lighthouse Service purposefully planted a bunch of saplings each year to keep a perfect mix of old and young trees. They were everywhere and acted as a natural wind barrier to our home.

At the crack of dawn on Christmas Day, the younger children from Reet (Rita) on down were spying out and sizing up their presents and guessing with endless possibilities what might be inside. They learned this little Christmas Day tradition (trick) from our dad!

Each Christmas before opening his presents, my father handled each one in a very careful and deliberate fashion, turning them around 360 degrees, squeezing the presents, and then offering an opinion about what was inside.

He had this uncanny knack of being correct about ninety percent of the time! How in the world he could predict what was inside his wrapped presents was beyond the rest of us, but it made for a fun family tradition nonetheless. This year was no different.

It was now around 7 a.m., and the rest of us joined in the Christmas day celebration and festivities. But first, we indulged in Mom's tasty egg and cheese casserole for breakfast, which we so looked forward to each year and were never disappointed by. That casserole, combined with a couple of delicious Thomas English Muffins, some home fries, and a splash of holiday eggnog, was so very satisfying to my palate.

So began a heart-warmed and love-filled day that would never be forgotten, whatever might come our way through the trials, tribulations, joys, and complexities of life.

One by one, Mom read the names on the presents and handed them out. We had a Clinch family tradition that each present had to be opened, time allowed for "semi-quick" admiring, and a proper thank you to the giver. This entire process usually took our family three to four hours, and it was an absolute joy!

Well ... back to that "semi-quick" admiring. I sensed that Mom and Dad had let things get a *tad little bit* out of control this Christmas! The orderly and controlled present-opening process had turned into a bit of unorganized bedlam! Oops!

I decided to firmly but lovingly encourage my siblings and said, "Come on, folks! We need to get this Christmas opening operation back on track! I want to make sure I remember this day as a wonderful event and not some crazed dogs ripping through a bunch of gifts!"

Mom agreed with me and stated, "Lola is right; we need to slow down and enjoy the moment. Let's try not to be quite as frenzied and rabid when opening the gifts."

Dad then put an end to the discussion by saying, "This is Christmas, and we need to be thoughtful with one another. I agree with your mother and Lola. Are there any questions?"

Case closed! That seemed to clear up any mass confusion about our approach to present opening the rest of the day!

We had just concluded the Christmas present opening marathon and were now moving on to our most important Christmas family tradition of all! We all took turns reading portions of the Christmas Story of Christ in the manger! The birth of a Savior!

However, just as we concluded the unwrapping of presents and before starting the Christmas story, Dad and Mom stopped us dead in our tracks and said they had a few "family gifts" they now wanted to share with us.

You want to talk about Christmas excitement and intrigue! The drum roll, please! Dad quickly departed the "fireplace room" and said he would be right back. The very first present he brought out was something he had made or invented that was absolutely genius. I certainly know where Albert gets his inventive ideas and genes from!

Remember that nifty little swimming pool or fishing hole in the naturally occurring inlet on the island? Well, Dad had figured out a way to make a complete *privacy gismo* when using the inlet as a washing-up spot.

Somehow, he bent and welded two metal circle shapes at the top and the bottom and then attached four pieces of six-foot-long and one-inch-thick wrought iron on either side in a square-like fashion that held it all together.

Mom, for her part in all of this, made a curtain that would enclose the entire *contraption* with cloth that wrapped around for complete and total privacy when bathing.

All we had to do was attach the cloth with the hooks Dad made and swing it around to completely enclose ourselves inside the bathing area.

The girls were overjoyed at the prospect of being able to clean up a little outside of our regularly scheduled bath time. The boys thought it an interesting invention but were perhaps not so giddy and excitable as the girls were about the present. We still had another four to five months to wait for the weather to warm up before we could "give it a whirl around."

Next, Mom took her turn and said she would be right back and went out of the fireplace room. Another tense moment of great anticipation ensued, waiting for our next big surprise!

Mom came riding through the hallway with a boy's blue bicycle with all the gadgets one might expect. It was awesome! Yes, it was a gift the boys would have to share, but it didn't bother them in the least. They could now take turns traversing the island *lickety-split*.

Mom wasn't quite done with her portion of the gift-giving. Next, she walked out with a girl's red bike with all the frilly accessories that made it our own. This was fantastical! Wow! While none of our presents were brand-new, store-bought things or anything of that nature, they were given in a spirit of love, and that was all that mattered. Now, don't get me wrong, I wouldn't mind a new store-bought present every once in a while, but that was not in the cards right now! Maybe someday?

Beyond being able to traverse the island in short order, the bikes were a great diversion from the monotony of island living and allowed us to get some much-needed exercise as well! They were fabulous gifts that checked all the boxes!

Dad mentioned he had one more little surprise for the older boys. One could only imagine what he had up his sleeve this time.

He brought out a 12-gauge shotgun. I never imagined in a million years that the older boys would show the kind of emotion they did in that moment. Even subdued Razor let out a high-spirited yelp!

They were simply overjoyed at the prospect of shooting down a few more creatures of the "air-borne" variety or any other vermin that might inadvertently pass by our tiny island homestead.

Okay, now I knew why Dad and Mr. Jed had asked to be alone the last time he was here. Mr. Jed was now complicit in the Clinch Christmas Day conspiracy and intrigue! He had helped Dad smuggle in a bunch of our Christmas presents under the cover of conversation! Very tricky! I was going to tuck that one away in my memory bank!

Along with the big gifts from Mom and Dad, the individual gifts were a blessing as well. All the individual gifts seemed to fit the personalities of the receivers with precision.

Clothes for Madelynn (Mad) and JoAnne (Jo-Jo), books for Albert (Al), knitting tools for me (Mumsy), fishing lures for Willie (Razor), a pocket watch for Teddy (Big Chief) that he could show off, a new Bible and clothes for Reet, and, well ... you get the idea!

The real twist that made this Christmas marvelously notable came a full two hours after the gift-giving event.

We noticed during our gift-giving exchange that Dad had purchased a used book for Mom as his gift to her. It was the Little Women classic written by our favorite, Louisa May Alcott. It was a very nice gift, but my father had something much bigger up his sleeve that he wanted to share with Mom.

Because I was so good at hiding my presents from the boys, Dad let me in on this secret weeks ago and asked me to hide his gift for

Mom until this very moment! While everyone was sitting in the fireplace room, Dad gave me a wink and a nod and whispered for me to go get the present.

I nonchalantly walked out of the room and went to fetch the gift. I went directly to where the gift was hidden. Well, I went directly to where I "thought" the gift was hidden! It wasn't there! I started to panic. I started rummaging through all of my drawers and hiding spots, and still no present. My stomach was in a knot right now!

At that point, I began talking to myself and said, "What in the world did I do with that present? I hide dozens of presents every year and can't believe this one is not where I put it. I wonder if somehow one of the boys might have found it and relocated it as a joke. No, that can't be it...."

Then it dawned on me. I had moved the gift from my original hiding spot to another much more secretive hiding place. I ended up putting it way in the back, away from the other presents on the mezzanine in Big Chief's lean-to! Because this gift was from Dad, I decided to push it way in the back and around a wooden crossbar. I had totally forgotten about it!

Fifteen minutes later, I showed up with the present. Dad had a very curious and puzzled look on his face but was relieved when he knew I had the gift! I decided not to spill the beans about my self-initiated silly little dilemma! Whew!

He quietly got everyone's attention and then pulled out a beautiful necklace that had a gemstone for each of her nine children and was emblazoned with the month and year they were born.

Dad very proudly stated, "Here ya go, Katy-girl. I love you!"

Mom was now all choked up and had tears pouring down her cheeks. She gave Dad a big hug while she sobbed uncontrollably. In my fifteen-year-old eyes, that seemed to have capped off a perfect Christmas Day!

The joy I saw that day cannot be described in words, but rather, it was a spirit of love that could only be understood by our heavenly spiritual desires, groanings, and anticipations.

Some call it an agape form of love through gift-giving. Well, whatever it was, the Clinch family experienced all of it, and we were *full to the brim* with love that wonderful Christmas Day!

8

A LONG, CRUEL, SILENT WINTER

WE BEGAN THE MONTH OF JANUARY IN 1914 WITH VERY HIGH spirits. Coming off the *extra-most-bestest* Thanksgiving and Christmas we'd ever had as a family, we were positive and optimistic and ready to conquer the world! The new year also started off with a monumental and "curious" BOOM, BANG, and POW!

Mom and Dad called us to the dinner table and made a very big announcement that third week of January in 1914, to the surprise and amazement of every one of us.

They announced that my father had once again walked by their bedpost and that our family would be blessed with another baby!

The emotions from us kids ran the gamut from surprise, happiness, enthusiasm, laughter, to absolute shock. Mom was in her mid-forties ... how could this be? Was that even possible? Well, I guess it was!

The boy's eyes were wide open and round with astonishment! The girls kept giving one another glances of wonder and curiosity back and forth across the table.

I finally asked the very first question, "Mom, do you think it will be a safe pregnancy? There won't be any worries, will there?"

Mom said, "No, sweetie, I am in very good health for my age, and the baby will be just fine. God allowed this wonderful blessing, and I am positive He will protect the both of us!"

Dad then said, in his quiet and unassuming manner, "We're all going to have to pitch in and help Mom over the next six or seven months. Having ten children is a very big responsibility and a blessing from God. It will be all hands on deck!"

We were going to have ten children in our family! You heard that right! Ten children! This too, changed everything!

When February rolled around, we got a bunch of sickness in our house. I hate to say it, but I thought Mr. Jed brought it with him during his last trip. He'd mentioned he had the sniffles and was feeling a little under the weather, probably not wanting to draw too much attention to himself. It went through our entire home like an untamed wildfire.

It was much more than *a little under-the-weather* sickness. This was a full-fledged "flu cyclone" ripping through our entire house. By the end of February, eight of eleven family members came down with flu-like symptoms. It was disgusting. We all felt disgusting.

This particular flu was a two-week prison sentence. It was all we could do to pull ourselves out of bed. Mom, Reet, and Al were the only survivors. The rest of us lay curled up in bed in the fetal position, whining, complaining, and routinely seeking refuge in the one toilet in our home. We were too sick to venture outside in the cold to use the privy.

One day, we were lined up four deep to get into the bathroom! We were all doing *a little jig* outside the bathroom door, trying to relieve the pain and discomfort of our bathroom plight! We were not happy campers!

On another dreadful day during the sickness episode, we had three different puke buckets being used all at the same time. The smell was horrific and made the rest of us run for cover!

By the time March rolled around, we were beside ourselves, bored stiff and going stir-crazy. The atmosphere in our home was not so good right now. Cabin fever, anyone? Everyone was a bit touchy and edgy about everything. Emotions were high!

Mom and Dad thought it wise for them to read a poem to us and have the entire family contemplate its meaning and application.

This was in addition to our daily Bible reading. They each took a turn reading the entire poem to us as a family. Guess they thought it *might take* with two complete read-throughs!

Before they began, Dad stated, "Your mom and I are not asking for input, comments, or discussion right now but only asking for serious reflection and consideration of the words in this poem."

> "In the bleak midwinter, frosty wind made moan.
> Earth stood hard as iron, water like a stone.
> Snow had fallen, snow on snow, snow on snow.
> In the bleak midwinter, long ago
> Our God, Heaven cannot hold Him, nor earth sustain
> Heaven and earth shall flee away when He comes to reign.
> In the bleak midwinter, a stable-place sufficed
> The Lord God Almighty, Jesus Christ.
> What can I give Him, poor as I am?
> If I were a shepherd, I would bring Him a lamb.
> If I were a Wise Man, I would do my part.
> Yet what I can I give Him, give my heart.
> Yet what I can I give Him, give my heart, my heart."
> ~ Christian Poet Christina Rossetti (1830–1894)

We all sat in silence for quite a long period of time, thinking about those words.

I immediately thought to myself, *While my sinful nature bemoans the long, silent, cruel winter months, my Savior reminds me of His sacrifice on the cross that brings joy, hope, and peace. That is what Christina Rossetti's poem means to me this winter!*

The one thing we were so looking forward to was our quarterly trip to the mainland. We couldn't wait to spend a day in Friendship, Maine, for that one-day reprieve from the monotony and tedium of island living and getting the winter behind us.

Just that morning, Big Chief and Razor got into a scuffle and started pushing one another back and forth. Dad had to quickly step in before it broke out into a full-blown fisticuff. They were two full-grown men now, and it could have turned into a *wicked* disaster. Evidently, Razor got up from the breakfast table to get a second glass of water, and Big Chief decided to pounce upon and confiscate his last piece of toast! Razor wasn't having any of it!

I was starting to empathize with Mrs. Almond Twitchell and her outright refusal and objection to living on the island. Then again, that wasn't my call.

Don't misunderstand me, I adored all of Franklin Island's intrigues and beauties but despised her solemn and harsh winter cruelties.

I had been praying up a storm about our seclusion dilemma, but so far, no answers. I needed to be patient.

Wait! Did I just say praying up a storm? No, I meant I had been praying very hard for the tide to turn in our home or something of that nature! Goodness gracious and *geewhizaciz*!

In the end, I trusted that God would take care of our family. All things work together for good for those who trust in Him. In God we trust! Much easier said than mastered, I must confess.

For whatever reason, when we first arrived in Friendship for our long-anticipated quarterly day outing, Dad asked to take leave of us for an hour or so. It was another one of those curious "Dad moves" that had all of us kids and Mom wondering again what he was up to. He had occasionally pulled this move before, and it usually meant he had something out of the ordinary up his sleeve.

Anyhoo, we looked forward to getting a little rest, relaxation, and some moments away from our island paradise to regroup, reenergize, and refocus our troubled spirits.

Mom and Dad, being the great parents they were, had specifically planned this quarterly trip on a Sunday with Mr. Jed so we could attend church. I think they realized our family had been desperately missing church and fellowship, even though we put on a church service on the island by ourselves.

It was getting close to 9 a.m. now, and Dad should be returning at any moment. Sunday School started at 9:30 a.m. and the main service at 11:00 a.m. We were a bit nervous about meeting a bunch of new people, but the need for fellowship was now overpowering those nerves, and we were all looking forward to church. Dad showed up at 9:10, expressionless as usual, and we walked the short distance to church.

Before church began, Pastor Gladwell met us at the door with a great big smile on his face.

He commented, "It is so good to see a family like yours wanting to spend time in the Lord's house. You are so very welcome! If there is anything we can do for you, please do not hesitate to ask. It is our pleasure to serve other brothers and sisters in Christ."

Mom responded, "Thank you, Pastor! It has been a while since we have been in a formal church building. We usually hold service on the island that my husband is responsible for. It's called Franklin Island. We greatly miss fellowship opportunities with other brothers and sisters in Christ. We hope to get more of that here!"

Pastor replied, "You will get plenty of that here, for sure!"

The people in this church were so friendly and hospitable. We shared with them all of our recent "goings-on" with all of our sicknesses and asked if they would pray for us.

The pastor immediately jumped into the conversation and said, "Our church wants to do much more than pray for your family; we want you to become members and be part of our church family!"

This was welcome news to my ears. It seemed God might be answering my prayers after all and was giving us a lifeline to the outside world! I must say this answer to prayer was timely and perfect!

While we would be attending this church on a sparse and semi-regular basis because of the accessibility and distance to the island, we now had people who would be praying for us and genuinely caring for us. This meant the world to our family.

After church, we were invited to stay and attend the afternoon lunch get-together. Each Sunday, all the moms put on a "potluck" afternoon lunch that lasted until 2 p.m. It was a great time to meet and greet everyone and get to know them on a more personal basis. The food was outstanding and the fellowship even better!

The people in this church truly seemed to be kindred spirits to our own. They were down-to-earth Christians with "no airs" and folks who wanted to serve the Lord and help others. Their sincerity and honesty were attractive.

The church was made up of about one hundred members from all walks of life. Young, old, newcomers, and charter members, the church had a good overall range of folks.

There were many varied personalities and vocations in this church as well. We had farmers, a long line of maritime workers, a restaurateur, various small business owners, and even a new kind of doctor I had never heard about before—a chiropractor—and his name was Doc Popwell.

Daniel David Palmer is credited with inventing chiropractic work and was responsible in part for Doc Popwell's glorious career in Friendship, Maine.

Mom said he adjusted patients' back alignments and sometimes cracked their bones back in place to relieve pain and pressure. She also said this particular type of doctoring service was invented about 20 years ago by a man named Daniel David Palmer.

We met another new family that afternoon, like our own, who had just moved down from New Brunswick, Canada. Their last name was *LaPierre*. The mother of the family was a single mom, as their father had recently divorced her a few months back.

She shared the heartbreaking story of what she and her two sons had been going through emotionally and spiritually while trying to survive. The oldest son was twenty-one, and his name was Emile. The youngest son was seventeen, and his name was Harold.

I noticed Emile had a very friendly countenance about him and had a great sense of humor. He wasn't shy either and came over and introduced himself to our entire family. Dad liked his sense of self-confidence.

Mrs. LaPierre wasn't planning on settling down in Friendship but had her sights set on the big city of Portland, where she was hoping to find a good job. For whatever reason, God providentially had them stop in Friendship for a few days to rest up before making the last leg of their journey.

While Mrs. LaPierre was speaking with us, someone overheard that she needed a job and mentioned a position was available over at the local restaurant if she was interested. The owner of the restaurant was Mr. McDonald, who happened to attend this church!

Mrs. LaPierre said, "Let me pray about it, give it some serious thought, talk it over with my two boys, and let Mr. McDonald know of our family's intentions. We are planning to move to Portland."

At the end of the two-hour potluck, we said our goodbyes to our new church family and headed off for a little shopping and sightseeing before jumping on board Mr. Jed's auto-boat back to Franklin Island. Dad asked us to get back to the Friendship Community Boat Launch about fifteen minutes early.

Okay, now I know that he had something secretive going on. First, he had gone off by himself for an entire hour, and now he wanted us to be back at the boat launch fifteen minutes early. None of the other kids thought a thing about it, but I was way too in tune with my parents' mannerisms to think nothing at all was going on!

I was much too aware, observant, and curious to let my father think he was *pulling the wool over my eyes*!

The other kids might be able to float and flit around unawares concerning the intrigue of the moment, but not me! He was definitely up to something!

At 4:45 p.m., Dad walked down to the boat launch carrying a basket with a covering over the top.

He then proceeded to make a matter-of-fact statement in typical Dad fashion, with little fanfare, when he said, "I thought we might take this little girl back home with us. I am told she needs a loving place to live with lots of kids."

Dad uncovered the basket, and out popped the cutest little dog I had ever laid my eyes on. What a precious little *whipper-snapper*. It was a two-month-old Golden Retriever with the happiest disposition. Since Dad had taken her out of the basket, she hadn't stopped her cute, uncontrollable wiggling, wagged her tail a mile a minute, and gave us endless kisses. We were all smitten with this precious little animal! Yippee!

Dad said, "I sensed we were all starting to get a touch of cabin fever and needed something to change up the mood and spirit in our family. I realize being confined to such a small space and on such a small island is starting to get to us."

I responded, "Thank you, Dad, for giving us the perfect solution for our sin-filled doldrums. This is fantastical!"

Mom added a funny little comment behind her smirk, "Does this mean that the next time we come to Friendly, I get to bring home a cat?!"

Most of the kids pounced on the feline comment and loved the idea!

I then decided to take the initiative and said, "This perfect little solution to our spiritual doldrums will be named Daisy! I think it fits her bright and cheery personality!"

Yes, Daisy was the newest addition to our family of eleven, soon to be twelve, with Mom due at the end of August with our new little sibling!

However, not everyone was sold on the name Daisy. The boys were leaning toward a less feminine-sounding name.

Razor and Big Chief suggested naming the dog with an Indian-like name. Something like Two-Coats or Bird-Feather or something of that nature. We decided to put it to a vote, and Daisy won out! Dad and Al sided with us girls to win the day in the dog-naming department. Daisy it was!

Two-Coats? Come on! Please!

The boat ride over to Franklin Island was a bunch of fun. We all took turns holding and loving on our new little bundle of joy. Our new dog Daisy was the absolute best, but we were encountering a small *tad little bit* of a problem!

I must admit I laughed out loud when Daisy deposited her first present right in Madelynn's lap, who was so very prim and proper and clothes happy! Boy, did she ever live up to her nickname, MAD! Mad was not a happy camper now that Daisy had unloaded her own little bundle of joy in her lap, and she was hopping mad!

The mess was everywhere, and it stinketh! Yuck! I was convinced the smell was the most sickening stench and the worst smell I had ever encountered in my entire life! We kids were now over-dramatizing the situation and giving MAD a bunch of nonstop "horse-laughs!"

Alright, alright, I was exaggerating again! But I had to ham it up a little for MAD to experience the full-frontal assault of Daisy's first gift.

A definite Clinch family memory book item and one we must move to the top of the list, post haste. It would be in complete honor of MAD, of course, and her *high muckety-muck* ways. Simply way too funny!

And, if I could be so bold to add, "The fly is in the ointment and it stinketh."

The ointment being that precious little Golden Retriever satisfying our need for something beyond the long, cruel, silent Maine winter, and the fly was the perfectly packaged, sloppy brown little gift from Daisy sitting on MAD's lap! Hee-hee!

9

CREATIVE ISLAND MINDS

ONE OF OUR VERY FIRST DISTRACTIONS THAT WINTER, notwithstanding Mom's curious and spectacular pregnancy announcement, was the mini- "ski-slalom" we put together on the back side of the island. By ski-slalom, I actually mean a 150-foot-long gentle slope about six feet wide between a bunch of stately spruce trees. We cleared endless amounts of brush and dead trees to give us just enough room for a running start and pushing ourselves to Olympic victory, glory, and gold!

I honestly thought a few of us were motivated and inspired in part by the great Norwegian skier and immigrant to America, Lars Haugen, who now lived in Maine. Lars won the National Skiing Jumping Championship a year ago in 1912, from what we read about in the sports section of the newspapers Mr. Jed brought us whenever he came.

Lars was muscular, athletic, and astonishingly handsome, drawing attention to the sport from both male and female soon-to-be avid skiers and jumpers!

We had some very old wooden cross-country skis we brought with us from Scarborough that were just perfect for such an occasion. Each and every time we got a dusting of new snow, we kids headed to "the mountain" for some competition.

If it was a big snowstorm, we brought our snow shovels to clear off just the right amount of snow to make it slippery enough for us to master the ski slope.

For competition purposes and bragging rights, we marked out the longest overall ski run as well as our individual personal bests for distance. I brought different colors of yarn, cut them into various lengths, and attached them to tree branches to identify the exact spots of our Olympic heroics.

We spent hours on end pushing one another down that silly, gentle slope. I think the boys enjoyed pushing us as fast as they could, hoping for a collision or a fall, but they were enthusiastic nonetheless in their desire to give everyone a great big send-off!

Of course, the older boys got the best jump and total distance, but it didn't matter. We were having an "island boat load" of family fun, and it got us out of the house and out from under our parents' noses for a few hours. But that wasn't all the Clinch family kids tried our hand at during our time on the island when attempting to have some clean, adventurous island fun!

Lars Haugen was a handsome Norwegian immigrant to the U.S. who won the National Ski Jump Championship in 1912. All of us Clinch family children followed him very closely.

Remember that "Franklin Island Fort" I briefly mentioned and prophesied about a little earlier? Well, that prophecy turned into a full-fledged reality! This was not just some child-like fort structure put together same-day for a creative fancy or something a couple of bored kids might throw together in an hour or two. Nope, we were talking about an elaborate monster fort with all the bells, whistles, and trimmings!

The first thing we did was spy out just the right combination of spruce trees that would give us the "solid foundation" on which the rest of the structure could be built. It also had to be as far away from the lighthouse as possible for privacy purposes, so the boys argued and convinced us of this.

I know what you are thinking! You are contemplating my earlier comments about Swiss Family Robinson or, in our case, the Clinch Family Survival outpost!

While the fort wasn't nearly as majestic, elaborate, or inventive as theirs, it was a labor of love, and we kids were determined to impress our mom and dad!

The incentive for building this Franklin Island Fort was staring us right in our faces for almost a year. Then, all of a sudden, the lights went off when the crusty decades-old boards jumped right up and bit us in our rear-rewards!

Over the years and decades, there were many iterations of the house on Franklin Island. From time to time, the U.S. Lighthouse Service would add rooms, renovate, construct auxiliary buildings, and once even did a complete rebuild of the premises.

Fortunately for us kids, they kept all of their excess lumber in a great big "pile" in back of the outhouse. Now, when I say great big pile of lumber, I was not exaggerating in the least little bit. It was massive. So we asked Dad about using the pile for building a fort, and he said he would check with the U.S. Lighthouse Service before giving us the go-ahead.

Our island lighthouse paradise sure had a bunch of changes over the years.

The U.S. Lighthouse Service left such a nice pile of lumber for us kids to build our Franklin Island Fort as a result of the many changes over the years!

Sure enough, their plans were to bring the wood to the dump "sometime" *down the road a piece*! Could anyone say, "Game on?!"

You want to talk about focused ... that we were! We made sure all the kids participated in this creative endeavor. We wanted to build a massive fort-like structure that we would be very proud of.

We asked Mom and Dad to wait until we were finished before they spied out our Swiss Family Robinson-style contraption, *sorta-*

kinda like the book did with their mom! We worked on that *little bug-ger* for an entire three months until we ran out of the free wood.

We started with four enormous spruce trees that created an almost perfect square at the base, about ten to twelve feet apart, and then figured out how to *jerry-rig* a quasi-hallway attachment to a couple more trees adjacent and off to the right another ten feet.

We wanted to build a multilayered structure so that Big Chief and Razor had their private space, we girls would have our own, and the rest of the boys could hang out in their own getaway. It was a three-floor masterpiece (so I self-proclaimed and imagined) with a hallway about ten feet in the air leading to another small room.

The room down at the end of the hall-like structure was the room Big Chief and Razor built for themselves. Razor indicated he was going to live in this room during the summer months.

While I thought staying in the room was a fun and adventurous idea at first, I was now not quite sure I wanted to see Razor pulling away from our family even more! I was so worried about his spiritual state that I was not sure more separation from the family was the answer. Between all the hunting he did and now using the fort as his "getaway" bedroom, we might never see him! I decided to run my fears by my mom.

I said, "Mom, are you sure it's such a good idea for Razor to live in the fort *all by his lonesome* during the summer months? Won't doing that further separate him from the family? He hardly says a word to any of us and seems to be pulling away from our family even more, and I am concerned."

Mom replied, "Lola, you are so very perceptive. Your dad and I have already had some discussions about this and will monitor just how much time he spends alone. We plan on making sure there is a nice balance between his need for adventure and being by himself with family time. Please continue to pray for Razor."

I ended, "Mom, I've been praying for Razor for quite some time now."

One of the special features of the Franklin Island Fort was the majestic lookout tower we built on the top of the third floor. We added a railing for safety so no one would fall and get themselves killed. It was a little tricky getting up there and was not for the faint of heart, but we attached a homemade ladder to the side of the fort as our way up to the roof.

We also had a backup exit from the roof with a very long piece of Hawser nautical rope Dad let us use. We even built a little mini pull-up ladder in the main quarters, which Razor had fastened together to keep any intruders out that might pass our way! One always had to be on the lookout for pesky neighbors! Hee-hee!

The view from the tower was an incredible one-of-a-kind view looking off to the north end of the island out over the Atlantic Ocean. Simply amazing! An image I couldn't get out of my head!

This is the Hauser nautical rope the Clinch children used in the construction of our lookout tower escape exit at the Franklin Island Fort.

The girls took extra measures to *gussy up* our room in the fort and added all kinds of frilly girlish things, driving the boys absolutely mad. Once we knew we were *getting their goats*, we added and embellished so many soft and girly colors, tapestries, and other knick-knacks that it was out of this world tasteless and gaudy!

But that was the point, now, wasn't it? Oh, what delights we girls were taking with our "creative designs!" Way too much fun driving the boys crazy-nuts!

When Mom and Dad saw the finished product, they were extremely impressed and proud of what we had accomplished.

Mom said with a wink and a smile, "I guess your dad and I will just have to give you an 'A+, 100-percent' grade for your shop and home economics classes, now, won't we?"

We responded with a bunch of hearty giggles and laughs.

Dad, being a man of very few words, said, "Impressive. Extremely impressive."

We had Mom and Dad's affirmation, and that was all we were looking for!

Then one Saturday afternoon, when the skies were blue, not a cloud in the sky, with very calm seas almost as still as glass, Dad proclaimed, "We are going to have a Clinch family competition!"

He stated, "We are going to have a solo rowboat race around the perimeter of the island. Whoever has the best time wins the prize. A prize to be determined at a later time."

We girls immediately knew we were in *a tad little bit* of trouble since the boys were a *mite bit* stronger than us, but we were excited at the thought of watching those crazy "he-men" duking it out on the ocean seas.

We decided to sit this one out and just cheer them on with gusto. Quite frankly, I didn't want to be a spoiled sport, but I had no interest at all in participating in this kind of event. I was one hundred pounds soaking wet on a good day, and the competition didn't suit me whatsoever.

First up was Big Chief. At six-feet three inches tall and 260 pounds, watching him flail away with those silly little oars was a sight for sore eyes. Teddy almost had that tiny rowboat swamped. Another six to eight inches down and the rowboat would have sunk!

He was making "some" decent progress, but by the sweat I saw pouring down his face, I knew that by the end of the race, he would be tuckered out, spent, and probably would run out of gas.

Sure enough, we saw him coming round the bend by the mooring, huffing and puffing with his tongue hanging halfway out of his mouth. Hilarius! Everyone in the family started yelling, screaming, and cheering him on to the finish line. He was soaking, ringing wet at the end.

He finished in twenty-five minutes and thirty-three seconds. Not bad for a very big guy with a very big ego. Well, on that particular day, that ego might have shrunk down a *teeny-weeny little bit*! Hee-hee!

Next up was Razor. I could tell just by looking in Razor's eyes that he was ready, and this competition was right up his alley! His six-foot, two-hundred-pound, wiry, lean frame was built for this kind of competition. He got off to a rousing start, alternating back and forth with the oars in a smooth and repetitive fashion and was soon long out of our sight.

Yup, *shore as shootin'*, fifteen minutes later Razor showed up at the mooring almost in the same condition as when he left. No huffing and puffing, no wagging of the tongue, and no parched tongue or lips. He was just digging into the ocean seas with vigor and determination with those oars so he could win this competition. Dad recorded his time at fifteen minutes and twenty-six seconds. Outstanding!

I gave him my typical Razor compliment and said, "Razor, you are an absolute beast!"

All the other boys, with the exception of Hocker, bailed out on the opportunity to have a go with the rowboat in Dad's newly initiated rowboat race. I think they realized they didn't stand a chance and that their turn would come a few years down the road.

Hocker, however, who was approaching fifteen, said, "I ain't no chicken gizzard coward, and I want to prove I can make it all the way around."

Dad gave him the green light but kept an eye on him as he traversed the perimeter of the island in the rowboat. He stayed just far enough out of Hocker's view, walking in between the thick spruce trees to avoid being seen.

Dad just wanted to make sure he was safe and okay in the rowboat. It took Hocker forty-four minutes and twelve seconds, but we cheered him on just as enthusiastically as we had for Big Chief and Razor.

On his way to the finish line, it seemed Hocker was so famished that he had to stop every minute or two to catch his breath and then row another ten or fifteen feet, only to rest once again. That brave, poor little soul, he looked exhausted but sure gave it *a good ole college try*!

Dad was the last one to attempt the rowboat challenge.

In somewhat of a half-joking fashion, I yelled, "Give it to 'em good, Dad, and show 'em who the real boss is!"

He lifted the oars very high in the air, pumped his fists up and down, and replied, "This race will be a piece of cake. I'll do it in under fifteen minutes, and then you will know who the real boss is. When I was in high school, I was an accomplished athlete, so hold on to your britches, everyone!"

Dad was being such a *rabble-rouser* right now, trying to *get our goats*. He couldn't win.

I never expected in a million years that Dad could beat either Razor or Big Chief in this race or that he would say the things he said in the way he said them!

I had never heard Dad boast like this before! He seemed like an awfully confident oarsman right now! I believed he must have caught a *silly thinking virus* with the way he was boasting and carrying on so!

I gave him one last fun little jeer and a snicker with a half bit of truth mixed in when I yelled, "Please be careful, older youth, and don't have a heart attack!"

Mom replied, "Amen to that."

I couldn't believe what I was seeing! Thirteen minutes later, my father was coming around the bend from the mooring location and headed to the finish line!

He had his head held way up high in a *proud-looking, stiff-necked position,* whistling some sort of tune and trying to act like the race was no big deal! It looked like he would beat Razor by a little under a minute! I just couldn't believe my eyes! He was a great athlete, after all!

All of us kids had our jaws on the ground right about now. Dad was *soaked to the gills*, sweat everywhere, but not breathing very hard! Every inch of his clothes was completely soaked, like he had just jumped into the ocean and taken a swim or something!

I thought to myself, "I sure hope he doesn't get dehydrated or sunstroke as a result of all that rowing and physical exertion."

Dad's time was fourteen minutes and nine seconds. He absolutely obliterated Razor's time!

Razor walked over and said, "Great job, Dad, you deserve the prize, whatever it ends up being."

I could tell that Dad was relishing in his victory!

That night at supper, Dad indicated that he had a "small announcement" to share with our family about his "tremendous and well-earned victory."

With a great big grin on his face from ear to ear, he said, "I hereby do relinquish my title as the winner of the Annual Clinch Family Rowboat Race to the rightful recipient, Razor Clinch."

We all looked very puzzled at his wily and unusual proclamation.

Dad elaborated, "When I was walking around the perimeter of the island keeping an eye on Hocker to make sure he was getting on okay during his turn at rowing, the thought occurred to me that the spruce trees were concealing my identity.

"I thought to myself that if I took the rowboat out of the water and pulled it to the other side by land more than halfway around the perimeter, I stood a chance to win, and no one could see me do it!

"Just before I put the rowboat in the bay on the other side, I very quickly jumped in the water to make it look like I was sweating profusely!"

Dad started howling, bending over with laughter at his clever little trick. The entire family joined in the hilarious fun and amusement, which seemed to go on for quite some time! What a prankster! He got us!

This was not the last prank my father would play on us kids either. I think this island living was helping Dad come out of his stoic and reserved island shell *a tad little bit*!

Later that summer, he decided he wanted to have a fishing derby. He thought it was a competition where everyone could participate, girls included. So we all got our fishing rods out and went to work trying to catch the biggest fish we could possibly catch. Most of us used worms and night crawlers we had dug up in the backyard near the outhouse, while Razor, Big Chief, and Dad were using their *fancy-schmancy* special kinds of fishing lures and those fishing-jigger *do-dads* or *whatchamacallums*.

Everyone was having a great time catching a bunch of fish and trying to win the *Clinch Family Annual Fishing Derby* when my father had one of his "dad prankster moments."

Out of the blue, he jumped into the rowboat and brought with him a fishing rod and a great big metal canister about three feet tall and sixteen inches in diameter.

With an emphatic tone and big trouble-making grin on his face, he exclaimed, "Well, I didn't establish any rules that you had to fish from the island shores, now did I?!"

He rowed out about thirty feet from the shore and dumped the contents of the canister into the ocean! It was shark chum! He took all the fish guts from the fish everyone caught that day and started chumming for sand sharks!

I simply couldn't believe my father! He was always trying to come up with an angle to win or, at the very least, to make us laugh, shaking our heads in disbelief. My dad was unique and a barrel of fun!

And, yes, the three-foot sand shark he caught was the biggest catch of the day! Go figure! That fun-loving, scheming little rascal, I loved him so!

The next family creative endeavor came when we got three feet of snow dumped on us with one of those fantastical, yet frequent, Maine Nor'easters. This time, however, it was my turn (Mumsy) to suggest a little family project!

With much enthusiasm and pride, I stated, "I have an idea! What do you think about building the biggest igloo imaginable now that we have all of this snow and it's so very cold outside?!"

In no time at all, the Clinch family members' wheels started turning, surmising and speculating about what this igloo design might look like. Razor had the *super-duper* idea to first build a small thirty-foot tunnel starting at our front porch before reaching the igloo. That way, we could quickly avoid that extremely cold wind chill factor sweeping across Franklin Island. We all thought that was a stupendous idea!

We got to work on the igloo that very same day and worked four to six hours a day off and on for two whole weeks. We were so very happy that the weather fully cooperated! *Thank you, God, for helping us out*!

We even used buckets of water from the house to "firm up" our blocks of snow with the ice created from the overnight freezing temperatures. It was so much fun to see our entire family participate in this igloo construction.

What else were we to do when buried in an avalanche of snow six nautical miles out in the middle of the Atlantic Ocean *all by our lonesome*?

At the conclusion of our two-week "igloo sabbatical," I stated with much wonderment, "This is a maritime masterpiece!"

These were just the "tip of the iceberg" of the things we got ourselves into as a family. There were things like Johnny Boy's newly created daredevil "bike jump," which *scared the living daylights* out of our parents, that would keep us entertained for hours; a newly crafted overhang enclosure that served as our resident combination bathhouse and fishing hole. We were able to construct and finagle the enclosure out and over the naturally occurring inlet for keeping the birds' poop out of our hair, to our delight, and other wondrous and creative joys that carried our days blissfully away.

10

THE CALM BEFORE
THE STORM

WE HAD BEEN BACK HOME FROM OUR QUARTERLY VISIT TO the mainland for about three weeks now. The weather had let up *a tad little bit*, our emotions had settled down, sicknesses were behind us, and we seemed to be getting along much better.

Daisy provided some much-needed comic relief and companionship and distracted me from any misery I might be self-imagining. All in all, it was going pretty well, and we were a month or so away from getting out from under this wretched winter weather.

This winter had been brutal! I couldn't decide which was worse: the amount of snow we got, the subarctic weather conditions, the frightful raging seas, or the pounding winds that took the wind chill factor to well below freezing for weeks on end!

Well, every bit of that was now in our rearview mirror, and I actually thought we were starting to get our "sea legs" back! Onward and upward!

We were about to eat lunch on the second day of April, the year of our Lord 1914. Stomachs were growling with envy at the sight of food! It was a little past noon, and Mom was making her customary noon-day trip to the second floor of the lighthouse to bring Dad his lunch.

It usually took her about ten minutes or so since our parents exchanged a few pleasantries and then got caught up on events of the day relating to us kids. Unfortunately, that sometimes took a little longer than normal. Oops!

Thirty-five minutes had now passed since she'd left with my father's lunch (which seemed a little odd to me). All of a sudden, he rushed into our kitchen with a frantic look on his face, like he had just seen a ghost. I had never seen Dad with such a worried look on his face as he had in this moment. Never!

Then he broke the news that Mom had just fallen halfway down the lighthouse stairs and was having some severe pains in her stomach. With tears flowing down his face, Dad asked us to pray for our mom and our new little sibling. He said this was a very serious fall!

Our entire family started crying and weeping. Some of us sobbed with a sound I had never heard before or since, while others had an intensity that seemed to yearn for the helping hand of Almighty God!

It was all happening so fast that our minds were racing with concern and love for both our mom and the baby.

With a very emotional and concerned voice, Big Chief immediately asked, "Dad, what can we do?"

Through his quiet sobs, Dad replied, "Your mom is resting in our bedroom and needs your prayers."

We all immediately circled around the kitchen table and bowed our heads in silence, begging God to deliver both Mom and the baby from any harm. My father seemed like a broken man. The stoic and reserved leader of our family had melted away into a devastated emotional mess. We had never seen our father cry like this before. Frankly, we had never seen him cry at all.

The big concern now was the medical attention my mom needed since we were more than six nautical miles away from any town doctor. We didn't have an auto-boat, and the little rowboat we did have to maneuver around the Franklin Island seashore wasn't equipped to make that kind of journey.

The very active, ominous, and raging seas would just not allow it in the violent headwaters of Muscongus Bay. It would be a self-imposed death sentence to try to navigate the bay with that rowboat!

I could see in Dad's face that he was panic-stricken to do something, anything at all, to get to shore and fetch a doctor. Honestly, I was worried he would try to take that stupid little rowboat and get himself killed!

Suddenly, little ten-year-old Albert, who had recently had a birthday, started praying out loud and said, "Dear God, please let one of the boats that my father warns with the lights from the lighthouse in Muscongus Bay come rescue my mom. Amen."

Out of the mouths of babes! What a great idea!

Could God be using little Albert to help save our mom?

Dad immediately went to the top of the lighthouse and started flashing S.O.S. messages to any boat that might be in the general area. From about 1 p.m. that day to midnight, he flashed some sort of distress signal he had learned during his initial lighthouse training, with absolutely no results at all.

In between times, he checked to see how both Mom and the baby were doing. The older kids also took turns checking on her to see if we could help with anything. She continued to have very bad cramping and steady bleeding that greatly concerned us, but, Mom being Mom, she assured us she would be fine.

She was getting weaker by the hour now, and we didn't know what to do. I didn't know how long she could keep hemorrhaging like this and survive! We were all very scared and concerned and continued to silently pray in earnest for her full recovery!

Johnny Boy was especially taking Mom's fall hard. While she would never admit such a "tall tale," Johnny Boy was her apparent favorite son, as he very rarely left her side. While his impetuous, risk-taking, and daredevil antics were usually front and center, when alone with Mom in our home, his softer side always became self-evident.

No one who was honest could refute that Mom and Johnny Boy were two peas in a pod and best buds. Some might say they were "double-walking" personalities: Mom with her fiery and disciplined personality and Johnny Boy with his fiery and determined need to be a risk taker and push the envelope. He was now lying in bed, sobbing uncontrollably.

Finally, at 2:35 a.m. in the early morning hours of the next day, Dad received a return signal reply from a nearby ship that confirmed our need for assistance. Thankfully, the ship that flashed us back was equipped with a small motorized dinghy of its own and could make its way to our Franklin Island mooring location. It wasn't easy, but they made it. The seas and swells were so violent that night that it took several attempts to anchor the dinghy. I just hoped they could get Mom safely into that dinghy!

The captain of the ship, Captain Davenport, was a very caring and gracious man. After he heard of Mom's circumstances, he had the greatest concern for her and wanted to help out in any way he could.

Dad, along with the Captain, a deckhand, and a few of the older Clinch boys, helped carry and carefully situate Mom in the motorized dinghy. It was taking much longer than we had hoped. The men were having great difficulty keeping their balance while trying to position our mom in the dinghy. They were trying to be gentle, but I noticed occasionally where Mom suddenly dropped down a foot or two, which seemed to knock her about. I just hoped she was okay!

When they finally got Mom settled in the dinghy after a terrible bout with the ocean swells, Dad said he was going with Mom to the mainland to get some help, and the rest of us kids would have to wait on the island for their return.

From what I could see through the binoculars I retrieved from Dad's office, the transfer of Mom from the motorized dinghy to the main ship went off without a hitch. There were many more men to help on the other end, which better stabilized our mom. They seemed to be taking good care of her and were being very gentle, attentive, and cautious. I was just praying all that jarring from loading her on the dinghy didn't further inflame the hemorrhaging. *Please God, take care of our mom!*

Our family would be forever indebted to Captain Jonathan Randall Davenport III for answering the distress signal that night. While he was a humble man who continued to downplay his role in the emergency, at the time, he was willing to answer the call, and that meant everything to us.

Before they left on the ship to Friendship, Dad said he would send word through Mr. Jed about Mom's condition if he couldn't do it himself in person.

All we could do now was wait, hope, and pray. The waiting was the difficult part. The hours seemed to drag on for an eternity. I didn't get to sleep until 4:30 a.m. in the wee hours and was up a few hours later getting the kids' breakfast ready.

We started our homeschooling routine about 10 a.m. with little to no progress. I decided to step up in Mom's absence and attempted to organize the day's assignments and pass out the schoolwork that needed to be accomplished. Al, Reet, and Mad were all very cooperative. However, the rest of the gang, not so much.

Big Chief flatly stated, "With all that is going on with our mother, I do not think today is a very good day to be doing schoolwork."

Razor added, "I am not doing schoolwork today, and that is final."

The other children decided to hold their tongue on the matter, but I could sense they did not want to do schoolwork either. The older boys might be correct. I needed to think about this calmly and coolly and from their individual perspectives.

Lord, what should I do? Please help me be the servant you want me to be!

After a few minutes of silent prayer, I gathered all the children together in the fireplace room to have a "chat."

I explained, "I think the boys might be right about starting school right away. What they were saying makes a whole lot of sense because of the tragedy. But I also think Mom and Dad would be very concerned if we didn't continue with our homeschooling fairly soon. As a family, we need to come to an agreement about when we will jump back into our studies. How about if we take today and tomorrow off and jump back in after that? Does that make sense to everyone? That will give us some time to get our heads on straight again."

Everyone liked the idea and was in agreement. It was amazing what could be accomplished when you asked for input into family decisions. I learned a valuable lesson that day. Instead of assuming things and telling people what to do, I should involve them and lead them to where they should be going. Shouldering this kind of family responsibility was a heavy weight. It helps me appreciate my parents' wisdom all the more!

About twelve noon, we heard Mr. Jed's foghorn go off, and we all went running down to the mooring as fast as we could.

With a calm and steady tone, Mr. Jed stated, "Your mom is safe and with a doctor right now and is being given a great deal of care. We will know more in the next twenty-four to forty-eight hours."

I latched on to his every word with an intensity like no other. All nine of us kids immediately started peppering him with questions all at the same time about Mom and the baby.

He then said, "Your father asked me to spend the night with you children to make sure you are all okay."

It was so nice to have an older adult around for the night, comforting us and allaying our fears. Mr. Jed was a very big blessing that day. He helped us carry in some extra firewood to cover the next week or so; helped with our supper; read some stories to the younger children; played a few board games with us to take our minds off our mom; and stayed up late, reassuring the older children that our mom would be okay.

Mr. Jed was much more than a business associate and someone indirectly connected to the U.S. Lighthouse Service; he was turning out to be a trusted friend, advisor, and confidante to our family. We were so very grateful to be able to call him our dear friend.

The other bit of good news came when he told us our new preacher man, Pastor Jeremiah Gladwell, and his wife, Joy, were planning to come out to the island for a few days to help out. They wanted to be an extra special blessing to our family during this very difficult time. The plan was for Mr. Jed to pick them up at 10:00 a.m. the next morning and ferry them back to Franklin Island around 10:30 a.m.

Our special Massachusetts friend was up before the crack of dawn, getting ready for the day's events. He beat me to the punch and already had the coffee brewing. Mr. Jed appeared to be a man of great discipline and routine, based on what I was observing. I offered to make him breakfast, but he declined, thanked me, and said he didn't eat a full breakfast and that coffee was plenty enough for him in the morning.

At nine o'clock sharp, he headed down to our mooring to jump on his auto-boat to meet Pastor Gladwell and his wife at the Friendship Community Boat Launch. He told us to expect to see them back at Franklin Island sometime between 11:00 and 11:15 a.m.

I must say that Daisy had been a sweetheart through all the pandemonium of the last few days. She was only five months old and seemed to be taking everything in stride. Fortunately, we remembered to feed this *little bugger* twice a day. The one time we were a little late with her food, all she did was become a little clingier until we fed her.

It was so nice to have a dog like her to hug and love on, especially right now. Golden Retrievers have the greatest dispositions and are simply the best. Did I already say that once or twice before? Well, it's true!

Anyhoo, all nine kids were working hard cleaning up the house before the Pastor and his wife showed up in a few hours. We wanted to make a good first impression and would hate for them to come and see a disorganized and unclean house that looked *like a bomb just went off*.

And believe me, with nine children, it didn't take long at all for those conditions to develop.

The girls and I made all the beds and dusted while the boys swept the entire house, including the lighthouse. We then began to chop up all the ice on the pathway from the mooring to the house. We were having an unusual cold stretch that April. The snow melted during the afternoon but froze again at night and in the early morning hours, which made for very slippery conditions.

I wondered now if that had something to do with Mom's fall? I hated to speculate, but it made perfect sense. Some moisture might have gotten trapped in small, unnoticeable portions of the stairwell and made for slippery conditions, unawares. Why else would she fall down stairs she had navigated a thousand times before?

I also decided to make a meal for the Pastor and his wife before they arrived. I began cooking a great big vat of spaghetti and meatballs over the open fire. This would be a piece of cake since I had watched Mom cook this meal many times before and even helped her out from time to time. Everything was going along just fine until I heard a loud hissing and bubbling sound coming from the vat. I was temporarily distracted when Jo-Jo asked for some help with her clothes and was preoccupied in the upstairs bedroom with her.

What a disaster! I should have known better. There was now tomato paste all over the stone encasement leading to the fireplace and all over the floor in the kitchenette. All I did was turn my back for a few minutes, and this happened. I just didn't know how Mom managed all of these house chores all at the same time. It reminded me of something Mr. Jed had mentioned once before.

He said, "Your mother is a very good organizer and motivator!"

Mr. Jed was right, and I needed to get me some of that!

Just before they arrived, we decided to jump in and help out, putting sand on the pathway so no one would get hurt from the mooring to our house. Dad and the boys had put together a nice stockpile of sand in the fall of last year in preparation for the long winter months and snowy weather conditions. I was sure glad they had prepared!

Mr. Jed's foghorn had just gone off, so we were headed down to meet our new guests. The tomato sauce mess in the kitchenette was almost cleaned up. I had to hurry!

11

HERE COMES THE SON

A S THE AUTO-BOAT APPROACHED, WE SAW MRS. JOY GLADWELL waving at us with gusto with her bright red handkerchief in tow. She had that hand of hers waving back and forth *a mile a minute*. She started making conversation with us about twenty feet from the mooring and seemed to have quite an upbeat personality. As soon as she got to shore, she gave each of us an extra-long hug and assured us Mom was in good hands and everything would work out just fine.

Talk about whirlwinds! This woman was an absolute Tasmanian buzzsaw, full of joy and optimism. I honestly was not sure if I had ever been around someone with this level of enthusiasm.

I had noticed her up-tempo'ed personality at the potluck dinner when we first met at church, but I didn't get a chance to spend a whole lot of time with her, as she was very busy serving and helping others and *bebopping around*. This woman could *talk the face off a monkey*!

I must admit I could take only so much of her hyper optimism right now. Don't get me wrong, I appreciated her willingness to help out but just wished she could tone it down an *incy wincy little bit*. I think it was making us uncomfortable. We all wanted to be at her level of excitability, but it was just not possible with what our mother was going through right now. I could tell that Big Chief and Razor felt a bit awkward.

Pastor Gladwell was no slouch either. He, too, was full of optimism and joy but didn't express himself quite as often or as persistently as his wife. The first thing he asked to do when getting off the auto-boat was to have a word of prayer.

It was a beautiful prayer that was prayed in a spirit of agape love (unconditional sacrificial love).

While I couldn't remember his exact words. He said something like, "God is in control, he loves his children, all things work together for good to those who love him and are called according to His purpose, and He is a God who cannot lie."

He then continued to say a special blessing and watch-care over the entire Clinch family and prayed that we would experience the full and complete love of God and healing through this tragic and unforeseen accident.

I truly wanted to believe what he was praying, but I had doubts. I wasn't able to have complete faith that God would protect my mom and the baby right now. I was letting anxiety and the responsibility of being the "second-Mom" distract me from my spiritual center. I was trying to do everything in the flesh, and it was just not working! Help!

Pastor Gladwell ended his prayer by acknowledging God's love, mercy, and grace. We had a couple staying with us who were full of godly wisdom, joy, and compassion, with a desire to help us and give us comfort. They truly loved us, and we had only known them for a short period of time. *Thank you, Lord!*

Pastor Gladwell and his wife knew their way around the kitchen and the fireplace too! While no one, and I mean no one, could beat our mom's cooking, I must admit that Mrs. Gladwell's cooking was tantalizing my senses right now! She made this incredible tray of Italian Lasagna and White Bean Salad to die for. It was absolutely *scrumpdillyicious*!

Oh, by the way, Mrs. Gladwell was able to salvage my spaghetti and meatball dinner! With a few tweaks here and there, she resuscitated "most' of my *big vat gone wrong*!

The boys were being *a tad bit* gluttonous, but the Pastor and his wife were more than willing to indulge their overly eager appetites under the circumstances. She made two large trays over the open fire, and the aroma was otherworldly. Mumsy (that would be me) gave the boys an "evil eye" to stop their gluttonous behavior, and it seemed to slow down their obnoxious table manners.

The next morning, Mrs. Gladwell outdid herself again with a seismic breakfast buffet spread. They brought with them bags of ingredients and groceries collected from the church members and local townspeople when they heard about our mom's fall. That was so very kind of them. Friendship was a wonderful community filled with caring and loving people!

The Pastor and his wife stayed for two full days and explained there would be a rotation of different husband-and-wife church members to come and help out while Mom and Dad stayed at the infirmary in town during her recovery. I couldn't believe it. An entire church family was wrapping their loving arms around a family in need when they didn't even know us very well. That was miraculous!

We obviously needed the help. With cleaning, cooking, and all the homeschool activities, things were in a bit of disarray. We needed a couple of steady and spiritual adult hands to guide us on our way.

The only passing negative thought and concern going through my hyper-tormented and worried mind right now was the amount of time Mom was spending at the town infirmary. It must be very serious if the plan was for her to spend an entire week or more away from her family. That was not like her at all. I was now wondering if we were getting "the rest of the story" or just enough for us kids not to worry?!

When I inquired further about this with Pastor Gladwell, he stated, "Your father will be home this Friday for a few hours to check in on you kids, give you an update on everything, and afterward will get back to staying with your mom. Don't you worry, everything will be okay because God is watching over your family."

I was so happy Dad would be home, even if only for a few hours. Next to Captain Davenport's reply to our S.O.S. call, that was simply the best news we'd had since this entire nightmare began.

It was Friday midmorning, and the attention-getting sound of Mr. Jed's foghorn rang like sweet music to our ears. Dad was home! We all sprinted to our Franklin Island mooring with reckless abandon, so determined to give our father the biggest bear hug imaginable.

He beat us to the punch! He grabbed each one of us and *squeezed the living daylights out of us*. It was so comforting to feel his loving embrace.

However, as he was loving on us and showing us his affection, I picked up a feeling or a look that something wasn't quite right. I couldn't put my finger on it yet, but something was off from his usual countenance and behavior.

The thought ran through my mind that maybe Dad was just overtired and exhausted from the events of the last four to five days, and he hadn't had time to catch his breath, get some normal rest, and fully recover. At least, that was what I hoped for.

After some brief small talk and getting caught up on the happenings on the island over the last few days, Dad said he needed everyone to gather around the kitchen dining table.

When Dad started, I immediately saw his facial expression change and his head slightly drop as tears started welling up in his eyes and flowing down his cheeks.

I started panicking, and it felt like a knife had just been thrust into the middle of my gut. So with great trepidation, I immediately rapid-fired my very anxious question and asked, "Dad, is Mom okay? Is she okay?"

With great emotion and a quivering voice, Dad said, "Your mom is doing better, but she had quite a difficult go of it the last few days. When she fell down the lighthouse stairs, she started bleeding internally. It was touch-and-go for a while, but God answered our prayers, and she is out of the woods now.

"The doctor and the nurse at the infirmary have been absolutely terrific. They have been a blessing. The one thing I have to tell you is that Mom lost the babies. They were not able to survive the fall, and both are in heaven with God right now."

At the end of his talk, he broke down and started crying out loud. We were devastated. We all started sobbing in our own personal ways of expression and heartbreak. A scene that would never be forgotten!

But what worried me even more was that this trial of life seemed to be swallowing my dad up beyond recognition. My heart bled for the restoration of his reserved and stoic personality that we all knew and loved. The despondency, anxiety, and worry had changed him in the last week to an unrecognizable version of himself, which we kids were trying very hard to understand and deal with.

We just didn't know what to say, what to do, or how to react. We instinctively said nothing at all once Dad broke the heart-wrenching news about the babies and just gave him one big group hug that lasted for a long while.

It was our way of telling him just how much we loved him.

Then I did something I had never done before… ever!

I decided to write down my thoughts, feelings, and emotions on paper. I suppose it was just a natural reflex and outpouring of emotion to relieve the intensity of my worry, distress, and anxiety. With paper and pencil in hand, I cried out to the Lord:

> Pain and sorrow are everywhere in this life-altering moment on Franklin Island. An indelible mark has now been etched on impressionable young minds and souls. The frightful circumstances which are never to be forgotten or removed. The cruelties and pangs of death lie all around and are everywhere.
>
> Let not the hope and aspiration of brighter days ahead be the endangered species of our tormented and hopeless minds but, rather, fill us this day with the certitude of your

divine presence and being, comforting our weary hearts, minds, and souls.

How shall us kids endure such pain? More importantly, how shall our mother and father leave such a trail of tears behind, moving onward to promises divine?

The unburdening of the soul is such a heavy weight to bear right now. The loss of two sweet, innocent young babes is more than we can handle all on our own. All excessive fleshly remedies are superfluous and lost in light of the transcendence of a holy and righteous Lord.

Only God knows the heartaches and struggles that lie ahead. We now fall prostrate at the feet of the Almighty, looking for answers, comfort, and hope sublime. The ordinary machinations of our flesh can't suffice in this very dark and dreary moment.

Lord, please come and rescue us. Please rescue our torn and ravaged hearts. Heal our sorrows and heal our wounds. Please come.

I didn't understand why, but I had to get it all out and put it down on paper. My worry, lack of faith, and questioning God's authority all came pouring out of me. How could God take care of our family in so many different ways but allow two innocent young babies to die? It just didn't make any sense.

I was so worried about Mom right now. She must be feeling a tremendous amount of pain with the loss of the twins. Because Mom was so early in her pregnancy and hadn't been to a doctor yet, she and Dad were unaware she was even going to have twins—a fact that added another layer of burden to our pain, heartbreak, sorrow, and now mourning. My heart was breaking for our entire family.

The next couple of hours were rather quiet as we tried to recover and process Dad's news and put on some semblance of normalcy for our father before he headed back to the mainland to be with Mom.

During this whole time, Mr. Jed waited patiently down at our mooring, book in hand. He understood the need for our family to be alone together and decided it was best to wait for Dad down there. A very considerate man, to be sure.

It was around noon before they headed back to Friendship, and we were sorry to see them go. Dad was hoping that Mom would be ready to come home in the next week or two.

In the meantime, after dropping off Dad, Mr. Jed would bring Mr. and Mrs. Pellegrin to stay with us for the next three days. When we first met them, they always seemed to have a smile on their faces. The amount of effort the townspeople were putting in to watch over us and care for us was *mindboggling* to me.

Two weeks had now passed, and the "Son" seemed to be rising fresh and anew. The love and care over the last two weeks was nothing short of amazing. Beyond all the church family members willing to give of their time, possessions, and love, we had seen additional activity to love on our family in ways no one saw coming.

The first thing to happen was the way the U.S. Lighthouse Service responded to our family tragedy. A beautiful bouquet of flowers and a heartfelt letter of condolence arrived at the infirmary.

They immediately said all fares back and forth from Friendship to Franklin Island in support of our mother's recovery would be covered by the State of Maine. That included all transportation for the next two months or more, if needed.

Additionally, the Executive Director told our father they would make an exception and allow for a total of six weeks' vacation time during the 1914 calendar year for Mom and Dad to have additional time to recover and have a bit more of a respite.

Next, they committed to having special stair-rails built for the spiral stairs going up and down the lighthouse structure to make it more safe and secure.

The last item surprised us the most. When a local politician heard of our tragedy, he immediately went to work investigating our situation to help out the best way he knew how.

He authored a piece of legislation in the Maine State Legislature that required each and every remote lighthouse under the care of the U.S. Lighthouse Service in Maine to be assigned an auto-boat on-site for safety purposes and access to the mainland, along with a monthly stipend for gas.

Word had it that when he stood up to give his speech in Augusta, Maine, about the proposed legislation, he roared with compassion and concern for our family and future families who would work and live on such remote island lighthouses. We were told there wasn't a dry eye in the Statehouse Chambers, especially after mentioning the loss of the twins due to our mom's fall!

Evidently, what pushed this measure well over the top and cemented its passage was politician Willie Thomas Haines' advocacy while on the campaign trail for the governorship of Maine. Haines was a very well-liked and powerful Republican politician who went on to become the 49th governor of Maine.

His obvious power and influence over equipping each remote lighthouse with a brand-new auto-boat impacted the vote in the end. There were no dissenting votes in either the House or the Senate in Maine. What a blessing!

Mom's tragedy was now known all around the entire State of Maine, with letters of condolence pouring in from everywhere. The letters spoke volumes about the compassion of Maine residents.

While we Maine folks could be a little rough around the edges, prickly, standoffish, opinionated, and a tad bit crass, when the rubber met the road, we were there for our neighbors in times of family emergency and crisis.

The people of Maine showed up in a very big way for my mom! At last count, we had over twelve hundred letters from people all over the state! Absolutely fantastical! God used other people to increase our faith!

We were so thankful to Willie Thomas Haines. He was the 49th Governor of Maine and was instrumental in helping to pass legislation assuring that each remote island lighthouse manned by a lighthouse keeper was equipped with an "auto-boat" on-site.

Thank you, God, for giving my mom and our family much-needed encouragement.

Jesus Christ our Lord, the "Son" of the Living God, demonstrated himself and came shining through in ways that couldn't be ignored, no matter how hard anyone tried to rationalize away the events of our mom's tragedy and her ensuing recovery.

12

GROWING STRONGER

SIX MONTHS HAD NOW PASSED, AND MUCH HAD TRANSPIRED IN our family. Mom continued to be on the mend. While physically the doctor had given her a clean bill of health about a month ago, I could tell that, emotionally, she was still a far cry from the person she once was. It made me wonder why God would allow this to happen. *Tell a lie*, it made me mad that He would allow this to happen!

I supposed events like the one she experienced did change a person for a very long time, and it would take much more prayer and reliance on God to get her completely through. With the way I was feeling right now spiritually, I could empathize with the spiritual mountain she would have to climb!

Other than the ever-present remnants of the devastating emotional turmoil and the longing and yearning for her twins, Mom was back in full force with her heavy hand of organization and discipline, keeping everyone in *ship-shape* and toeing the line. Homeschooling was back stronger than ever, keeping us focused while the upcoming fall season was once again staring us right in the face.

However, I was very concerned that her excessive discipline could, in part, be tied to her mourning and loss. I decided to ask Dad what he thought about it.

"Dad, is Mom okay? She seems a bit more aggressive with us children since she's been back, and the homeschooling is beginning to feel more like a reform school. I'm just very worried about her right now. Is there anything I can do to relieve the pressure on her? I want to be a help."

Dad responded, "Your mother is going through a very difficult mourning period. She is having a bunch of ups and downs and in-between emotions. The best thing for you to do is go to her and ask if you can help her. Be kind, gentle, and loving in your approach. Ask her how she is feeling since the loss of the babies. The more opportunities she has to *get it all out,* the better."

So I did exactly as Dad suggested, and I was glad I did. It seemed to lighten the tension between Mom and the rest of the family. If nothing else, she became aware of how others were feeling around her of late.

Mom had also been busy in the letter-writing department. She decided to write a letter back to every single person who had sent her a letter of condolence for the loss of the twins. She would include a gospel tract and a few kind words of encouragement in each letter.

It was her way of saying thank you while being a good testimony. She carved out an hour each day for her letter-writing campaign. For whatever reason, I think God was using this as a way of healing. It seemed to be very therapeutic for her to correspond in this fashion.

I had seen some tremendous growth in all of our family members. I was not sure one could go through what we went through and not be impacted in a maturing and life-altering way. Madelynn had especially stepped up to the plate. It seemed as though she had taken the role of "third-Mom." She was more consistent with helping out around the house and was always looking for opportunities to serve others. She had even taken the initiative to cook an entire meal by herself last week, with a little help from me. I was so very impressed with the way Mad was maturing.

One of the best outcomes (if there even could be) of Mom's horrible accident was our ability to now attend church every single week! The brand-new auto-boat assigned to Franklin Island lighthouse by the U.S. Lighthouse Service through the State of Maine was delivered a few days after she got home from the infirmary. Such a blessing!

Every Sunday morning, we got to go to Sunday School and then hear the preaching of God's Word in the main church service hour! Afterward, the "potluck dinner" the church put on allowed us to fellowship with other believers. I enjoyed Pastor Gladwell's messages from the Bible. The church had added quite a few additional members since we last attended, and it was growing!

Mrs. LaPierre and her two boys had decided to stay in Friendship after all, due to her job offer at the local restaurant, while her boys, Emile and Harold, started a job working for a construction outfit in the area a few weeks later. With the three of them now working, it had afforded them the perfect opportunity to move into a nice little, comfortable home.

Well, about that LaPierre family. I suppose I should *fess up* and say Emile LaPierre was showing me quite a bit of attention of late. If I'm completely honest, probably much more than I wanted right now. He was a nice guy and all that, but I was just not feeling it. I always tried to be pleasant to everyone I met, but I purposefully kept him at arm's length for fear he would think I was interested, which I was not.

The girls and a few of the boys had been teasing me unmercifully about Emile, and I told them in no uncertain terms to knock it off. I threatened to cut them off with the gifts from my knitting, and they decided to relent, post haste!

We kids were a year older now. I simply couldn't believe I was now 16 years old. Mom and Dad had gotten married when they were 16. *Mind you*, I was having none of that early marriage nonsense. That was just not for me. I planned on working, saving up some money, and traveling a little bit before committing and settling down with a husband and young ones.

Mr. Jed shared some more worrisome news from government circles. A major conflict had broken out on June 28th of this year, when the Archduke Franz Ferdinand of Austria-Hungary was assassinated. This had led to a formal Declaration of War a month later, on July 28, 1914. Evidently, a bunch of countries were involved. So far, America was not involved, for which I was very thankful.

I was worried sick that my older brothers would join the military. I couldn't imagine seeing two country boys from Maine leaving Franklin Island to fight an overseas war all alone and so far from home. *Lord, I know that your plan is perfect, but please protect my older brothers and give me a deep and abiding faith.*

Both Big Chief and Razor were persistent in their intent to join the Army. They wanted to serve and protect our country, should the United States become involved in a global war.

I prayed this wouldn't happen! War could destroy both individuals and families, and we had been through quite enough these last few months. But I knew the boys and their personalities, and they would do what they had to if that time should ever arrive.

Mom and Dad tried to downplay their involvement in any such war without coming right out and directly saying no. They realized it was ultimately their choice as young adults.

Our beautiful Golden Retriever, Daisy, was growing leaps and bounds and was truly one of the best dogs in the whole wide world! She was obedient, fun, and had a quirky personality, but in a good way. She sometimes kept us in stitches with some of her antics.

I must confess she had taken a special liking to Razor. They seemed to be extra best buds. Most every morning at 7 a.m., come rain or shine, with the exception of Sundays (Dad's rules), when Razor headed to the back side of the island to go hunting for ducks, Daisy was right there beside him. She spent a *goodly* portion of the day with Razor, fetching the birds that he shot or just hanging out with him when fishing. She was a great bird dog and companion.

I loved to watch her freeze, crouch, and fetch the game the few times I had accompanied them while hunting. Razor had been diligently training Daisy in the waterfowl "arts." She was a natural. Once Razor shot the waterfowl, she immediately jumped into the ocean or scoured the shoreline looking for that night's dinner. She was a very talented swimmer who never seemed to get exhausted.

It did concern me that Razor's hunting activity took him away from our family for long stretches of time. He spent more time alone with Daisy now than he did with our family. He was withdrawn and didn't seem to express any spiritual sensitivities whatsoever. I continued to pray for my brother!

When Daisy came in for the evening from a long day's hunt with Razor, then the rest of us got to play with her. She had boundless energy for such a young dog and was always ready to play and rough-house nonstop.

On September 1, 1914, our family was about ready to sit down at the kitchen table for our supper when we got a knock at our front door. Who in the world could this be?

It wasn't like we had any neighbors who just might be popping by to say hello or asking to borrow some sugar or a can of beans! All eleven of us got real curious real fast, while the older boys wanted to make extra sure it wasn't some crackpot or two casing the place for a robbery.

Dad slowly opened the door to two young teenagers about my age (16) who looked tired and scared. The boy's name was Tom, and his girlfriend's name was Rosie.

While Tom tried to maintain an air of self-confidence and maturity, the truth was that they both looked very shaken up, extremely disheveled, and *scared to death*.

I introduced myself first and said, "Hi, my name is Lola, and it's a pleasure to meet you both." I then engaged in some small talk and friendly banter to make them feel as welcome and at home as possible.

Because I was so self-aware and self-conscious, I couldn't believe how forward I was being with our guests. It just wasn't like me at all. I wondered if I might be getting beyond that socially awkward stage. Boy, I sure hoped so! It was amazing that I didn't turn three shades of red when conversing with Tom! Unbelievable!

I had a flashback to when Mom had lost the twins and how caring all the townspeople were, and I sensed that Tom and Rosie needed that same amount of love and attention right now. It was now our turn to help two fellow Mainers in need, and I was praying we could be a special blessing to them.

Tom and Rosie shared their horrifying sailboat story with us and expressed that they were just not comfortable about making another attempt at navigating that sailboat back home. They thought it best left for Tom's father to sail it back. I didn't blame them a bit. Being out to sea for two full days with little to no food or water and not knowing if they would survive was unimaginable to me!

Tom acknowledged he had sailed many times before with his father. However, when he and Rosie got caught in the extremely heavy winds and ghastly Atlantic currents over the last few days, he realized he was in way over his head and couldn't handle the sailboat.

He said his father warned him about staying very close to shore and keeping an eye on the weather, but he admitted he didn't listen and ended up way too far off course and out to sea.

I guessed he was trying to show off for his girlfriend while biting off a lot more than he could chew in the process.

Tom said that after a couple of hours of trying to navigate the sailboat, he became physically exhausted when turning the winches to hoist the sails, trimming and managing the heavy line, reefing in the very heavy winds, looking after the spinnaker sail, and attempting to steer all at the same time. He said Rosie was a very big help, but he just could not handle the intensity and physicality of what was required.

Tom commented, "I tried to rest every ten to fifteen minutes and then give the sailboat another try. This went on for about nine hours before I became so dehydrated that I was unable to continue. The little water we did bring with us gave me just enough fluids and energy to stay conscious, but we both realized if I continued to fight the severe winds and the intense Atlantic Ocean and Muscongus Bay tidal currents to get this sailboat under control, I would simply pass out or worse.

"Rosie and I both agreed it was best to let the sailboat go and take us where it was going to take us until the winds and the seas calmed down. We began to pray and ask God to get us back to shore safely."

At this point in the conversation, Dad chipped in with his understanding of the wind and water current patterns along the Maine Coast. As a lighthouse keeper, it was mandatory for him to have some informal training and a good working knowledge of the various types of weather patterns as he helped guide water vessels to safety.

Dad said, "A big part of my job is to observe and record the weather conditions for the U.S. Lighthouse Service and the State of Maine. This helps me operate the fog signals, a job requirement that needs diligent attention during foggy periods and with other types of bad weather.

"Years ago, lighthouse 'wickies' were prone to relying too much on personal judgment, but lately, we are being trained with a system of established rules that takes more of the guesswork out of the equation. The *fancy-schmancy* folks call them protocols."

Tom briefly jumped in and quipped, "Yuh, I guess I relied too much on my own personal judgment the last few days and did not listen to people like my dad, who were much more experienced and knowledgeable with sailboats than I was. I should have been 'prone to call' and listened to my father!"

Dad replied, "Don't beat yourself up too bad, son. Life is a learning process, and as long as you have learned a valuable lesson, you'll be okay."

Dad concluded by saying that the reason the good Lord had them land on Franklin Island from their original Wiscasset boat launch was because of the water currents this week, which were flowing in a north-easterly direction.

When Dad, who didn't usually speak a whole lot in public or in groups, was finished, I had an entirely new appreciation for what he did at work. It was much more than simply light on, light off. A lot more was going on behind the scenes in that lighthouse than I was ever aware of. But more importantly, a lot more seemed to be going on behind the scenes with our dad. He seemed to be changing toward having more of an out-front leadership role than behind the scenes. I was happy to see the changes in his outspokenness.

After supper, we asked Tom and Rosie to play a few board games with the family, and I think that it cheered them up a bit and put their minds at ease. I could tell that the worry on their faces started disappearing.

These young folks were so appreciative of the hospitality that our family was extending that they couldn't stop thanking us. What started out as a friendly date between boyfriend and girlfriend had turned into a harrowing ordeal, and they feared for their lives. So much for that dating stuff! No thanks!

As we got to know them a little better that night, we found out they were members over at the First Congregational Church of Wiscasset, Maine, which was one of the oldest churches in that town, dating back to 1752. It was nice to know we were helping some young folks who knew the Lord as their Savior!

Rosie commented, "We knew everything was going to be alright and that God would take care of us when we read the letter on your front door. We noticed your dad's letter and all the signatures at the bottom and instantly knew you were the kind of family who would help people like us in need."

At that point, I saw Dad get up from the kitchen table and scurry out of the room in a very determined manner. I didn't know with absolute one-hundred percent certainty, but I think their testimony about his Franklin Island Compact letter might have gotten him *a tad bit* emotional! This was an absolutely astounding thing to see from our dad in normal everyday circumstances.

Dad seemed to be changing and growing stronger by the day. I could honestly say the same thing for the rest of us. Mom, most of the boys, and all of us girls seemed to be growing stronger as individuals as we put our faith and trust in God. All the circumstances of the untimely death of the twins had helped us grow in ways we would not have considered. While I was thankful for the growth, I would prefer the faces of those two innocent young ones. *God only knows.*

13

OUR BROTHERS' DILEMMA

MANY FAMILIES GO THROUGH AND EXPERIENCE WHAT MY TWO older brothers were experiencing right now. Big Chief was in his nineteenth year, and Razor was about to turn eighteen. They both were very spirited brothers in their own unique and different ways, but they both had hearts of gold.

They had exterior personas that made them who they were, but deep down inside, I had been able to experience the love, joy, and happiness of their true inner selves. I loved my older brothers dearly.

Big Chief had a larger-than-life personality and was so full of natural charisma that I often wondered where he got it from. He could spin a yarn and embellish any situation, anytime, and anywhere.

If it added one bit to his exterior persona or directly or indirectly inflated his already insatiable and oversized ego, he was going to let it rip.

His largeness, either real or perceived, had allowed him to be in positions of authority and leadership his entire life. This included athletics, school-related activities, teenage money-making opportunities through odd jobs, or anything else he tried his hand at.

On the other hand, his brash, confident, and self-aggrandizing exterior also had the impact of putting off others who couldn't stand to be around someone with all that bravado.

So Big Chief had a mixed bag of admirers and detractors, depending on how gracious and amenable one was toward his outsized presence.

What people didn't experience from Big Chief was his natural kindness and generosity, which I had experienced my entire life. He would give you *the shirt off his back* and not think twice about it.

All my life, Big Chief asked, "Mumsy, how are you doing? Everything okay, Sis?"

It was his way of telling me that he loved me and wanted the best for me. And, if you want to talk about a protective older brother, Big Chief was the quintessential example of that. No one ever thought twice about messing with Lola, his little sister! Not happening, no how, no way!

It was comforting to know he had my back. Being six feet three inches tall and weighing two hundred and sixty pounds didn't hurt either. For some reason, big, tall people like Big Chief always seemed able to carve out a healthy dose of respect, whether they deserved it or not. My brother Teddy deserved it ... big ego and all!

I did wonder who would have my back when Big Chief left the nest. Would I be able to lean on and confide in anyone in our family during tough times? I had sure grown accustomed to a protector! Perhaps God was telling me I needed to rely more on Him in the first place!

Razor, on the other hand, was your prototypical introvert. You know, like the classical introverts and strong, silent types you read about in all those *fancy-schmancy, highfalutin,* and *high muckety-muck* novels and books everyone talked about. He kept everything all bottled up inside. You didn't hear much from Razor except when it came to his hunting and fishing passions and expeditions.

Most generally, all you got from Razor was yes, ma'am, no ma'am, yes sir, no sir, or some other very short and to the point response. On the other hand, he absolutely thrived in the great outdoors.

For Razor, his perfect day was a fishing rod in one hand, a 12-gauge shotgun in the other, with Golden Retriever Daisy by his side.

He was a simple man who went out of his way to stay out of everyone else's business.

His favorite expression that I had heard a thousand and one times growing up was, "It ain't none of mine."

It was Razor's way of saying, "Just go ahead and do your own thing and what you think is right because it's your business and not mine."

Unfortunately, I was not quite sure where he stood with the Lord, either. The only outward expression he had shown of anything spiritual was the one time when we first moved to Franklin Island, and our father asked us to each individually pray about signing the Franklin Island Compact.

Razor waited a full two weeks after it was posted before he finally put his name on that letter. The rest of us inked our signature the same day or thereabouts.

Quite frankly, I didn't know what to make of his delay in signing the letter. But overall, I was concerned with my second-oldest brother's spiritual well-being. It broke my heart to think Razor might not be one of God's own. I was praying for his salvation or for some indication that he knew the Lord.

Don't get me wrong, out of respect to my parents, Razor always participated in family activities that had a spiritual bent; however, as far as a personal relationship with Almighty God, I couldn't venture to judge.

One thing I did know was that Razor was protective of his family members, his true-blue Maine identity, and being a citizen of the United States of America. He was extremely protective and patriotic in this regard. He was a rugged and handsome outdoorsman who stood six feet tall and two hundred pounds. He was very strong and could outrun and outlift anyone in our family, including our father.

My favorite way of teasing Razor was to say, "Razor, you are an absolute beast," when it came to any of his outdoor hunting and fishing heroics!

Both of my brothers had started to grow *a tad bit* antsy of late, and I could tell they wanted to get out from underfoot. They were yearning for their individual freedom and wanted to spread their wings and leave the "Franklin Island nesting grounds."

It had nothing at all to do with Mom and Dad or the island itself. It had everything to do with their individual desires to be on their own. While I could completely understand, I was just not quite there yet. I still had some growing up to do before I got to that point. *God only knows.*

Each of the boys had already shown signs that they wanted to make decisions all on their own. The very first major indication came with all of their talk about joining the Army if the United States should ever get involved in a world war. They were both adamant about joining should the opportunity present itself.

Then, from time to time, they headed off together when we ventured to the mainland for supplies or some other occasion that didn't necessarily involve them. They *moseyed on over* to an adjacent town for a meet and greet with the locals, which included some females their own ages as well. They talked about the different girls they met during their "freedom excursions" but never brought one home to meet Mom, Dad, and the rest of us kids.

I think they both knew they were much too immature to attempt anything like a serious relationship right now. There was plenty of time for that *down the road a piece.*

Teddy (Big Chief) recently started being more aggressive at the supper table by taking alternative or opposing positions on issues discussed. Not sure I agreed with everything he was saying, but he sure tried hard, seemed to stay competitive, and held his own!

During one specific conversation at our supper table, everything seemed to change for Teddy. The conversation took a turn to a subject that was right up his alley. It was a simple business discussion about management and labor. Teddy took control and started driving the discussion hard! He was very articulate in his support of the rights of Maine workers and their determination to unionize. He had all kinds of facts and figures to support his position. His knowledge of the subject took me aback, but even more impressive was the way he spoke with such clarity and commanded a presence when speaking. I realized right then that Teddy could handle himself and got a glimpse of why he wanted some independence.

Razor, on the other hand, just shrugged his shoulders and gave us his patented, "It ain't none of mine."

It was January 2, 1915, when the freedom train finally hit the tracks for real with my two older brothers. They called for a private meeting with my parents to discuss their desire to be on their own. Teddy gave Mumsy (that would be me) a heads up about what they would discuss with Mom and Dad and asked if I had any advice.

I immediately thought to myself in that moment, *Now that is a hot potato that is much too hot for me to handle! I do not want to get into the middle of that family discussion.*

I certainly did not want either of my two brothers saying, "Well, Lola said this or Lola said that."

So I responded, "Speak from the heart and ask Mom and Dad to pray before the meeting begins."

That was all I felt compelled to offer. If being in a large family had taught me one thing, it was to be very careful with my words because the entire Franklin Island community would become delightfully aware of them before the day's end! And that could mean getting yourself into a heap of trouble or, at the very least, being put in a compromising position.

Both Big Chief and Razor outlined their plans to move to Portland, Maine, to get a job and then seek a small apartment for the two of them. They would be temporarily staying with friends from Scarborough while looking for employment. Teddy mentioned there was a very good local church in the area where they could meet good Christian people. Teddy did all the talking, with Razor cheering him on from the sidelines and agreeing with everything he said! Typical Razor!

Mom and Dad were okay with the plan but hated to see them leave. No doubt it would put a giant hole in their hearts for a while, getting used to the absence of their two oldest children. However, it didn't come as a total surprise to them since they were two grown men now.

Nonetheless, it was a sign for them that things would start changing in the Clinch family, which had my parents inwardly concerned. A natural concern that all families go through sooner or later. For my parents, it was sooner than they had wished or hoped for.

I remembered the day the two older boys left our Franklin Island "nest" (mooring) like it was yesterday. Big Chief and Razor said their "so-longs," packed their things in the auto-boat, and Dad sped off to Friendship so they could catch their train from Wiscasset to Portland.

It wasn't an overly emotional sendoff, with the exception of our mother. She did have to catch herself from sobbing two or three times, but other than that, it was a very happy sendoff filled with well-wishes, love, and God's speed. We watched our two older brothers speed away—one a commanding presence and protector (Big Chief) and the other a loner and a provider of game (Razor). I loved them both. Those were the thoughts that crossed my mind in that moment.

14

THE PURSUIT

OUR FAMILY HAD STARTED TO ADJUST TO THE ABSENCE OF OUR two older brothers, dividing the workload the best we could. I sure did miss all the waterfowl Razor would bring home on a nightly basis but was very careful not to say it too loud around Hocker, who was now seventeen and attempting to take Razor's place on the "big-boy" hunting roster.

Dad had been accompanying Hocker on his hunting expeditions to give him some informal fatherly hunter safety training and other pointers.

He was not anywhere near "Razor status" quite yet, but Hocker had been bringing home some tasty game now and again. We did have a three-week dry spell where he was coming up empty on the wild game front. But Dad took him aside, gave him some hunting pointers, and he seemed to be doing a bit better of late. Hats off to seventeen-year-old Hocker for stepping up to the dinner plate! Bravo, young man! You had some very big shoes to fill!

He was also benefiting significantly in the "mutt department" after taking over for Razor, now that he had complete and total access to beautiful and well-behaved Daisy on a regular basis!

We had been extremely active in the local church in Friendship these last few months. I counted it a blessing and a joy. It had become the "cornerstone" of our lives.

We constantly visited other families at their homes or invited them to Franklin Island for a day of fellowship and exciting, unknown adventure at our own!

We had such an appreciation for everyone in the church and the ministries they were involved with. It was so true that when everyone used their spiritual gifts for the church, the church became vibrant and grew organically.

This very same thing was happening within our own church. We were up to 150 members now, and Pastor seemed to be announcing new members all the time!

I had picked up a very persistent shadow at church of late! A shadow that had appeared on and off over the last couple of years. Yes, Emile LaPierre was just not going away. While I was only "slightly" warming up to his persistent and charming advances, I admit that I gave him an "A+ 100 percent" for not giving up. I wished I shared his level of enthusiasm, but I just didn't. I just wished he would back off! I didn't want to deal with all the attention right now.

Don't get me wrong, I thought he had many very redeeming qualities and all of that, but I was just not ready to settle down in that way. I had way too much to do before embarking on that sort of lifelong journey.

Emile was no doubt industrious, self-confident, caring, and very concerned for the welfare of his mom and younger brother, but I was not totally convinced that church was ultra-important to him. At least not in the way I had been raised to think about church and the free gift of salvation.

What concerned me most was the way he talked, with a lot of worldly expressions and rough-and-tumble jargon. We were eating together at a potluck dinner at church and making small talk when out popped a swear word that seemed as natural as could be. He immediately apologized for his misstep, but the situation continued to bother me greatly.

The LaPierre family initially came to Friendship Baptist Church as a temporary measure to grieve over the loss of their father as a result of his divorce from their mom, with the intention of eventually traveling to Portland to settle down.

Then God changed their plans when Mrs. LaPierre received a job offer in Friendship at the local restaurant and decided to settle down here. God did have a way of changing things up when we least expected it.

Franklin Island and all that came with it was a case in point. No way and no how would I ever have imagined when we were living on the mainland in Scarborough a few years back that I would be living on a remote island right now!

We saw Mrs. LaPierre on a regular basis at church, but the two boys (Emile and Harold) on a less frequent basis, and that was a total deal breaker for me.

Anyhoo, after our church afternoon "potluck" lunch one Sunday, I did "give in" to an ice-cream cone outing with Emile when he actually showed up for a service! I was not sure why I did, perhaps a little curious. He was very charming but just seemed to be a tad-bit worldly to me.

His construction job took him up and down the coast of Maine and kept him away from home with a rough and tumble crowd most of the time. Those construction guys were mouthy, worldly, and rough around the edges, and it seemed to be rubbing off on Emile in some small and subtle ways.

Who cares! He is not my boyfriend and not my son! I certainly will pray for him as a brother in Christ, but that's it, I adamantly and convincingly expressed to myself!

Mom and I had "a talk" a few years back when Emile first showed up on the scene and was expressing some interest. She kept her mother-daughter talk really simple.

She said, "Once a person is saved, virtue, consistency, and involvement in a local church are vital ingredients of a successful life."

I knew she was right. She was always hovering over the right spiritual targets, and I really did pay attention, whether I was feeling like it in the moment or not.

I replied, "Thanks, Mom, for your lifelong commitment to guiding us kids. I have never forgotten how you faithfully managed the loss of the twins but continued to love us unconditionally and help provide for our needs and give us direction. Your faith is real."

After a few more friend dates, I realized things were ratcheting up in his mind and I had to have an honest talk with "Mr. Emile." I had to tell him there was no chance I'd commit to anyone before I had achieved a few of my life goals of working and being on my own.

I pondered, *I do not want to go from Mom and Dad taking care of me to Emile LaPierre taking care of me. That would be too much, too overwhelming, and too restricting for me. I am not saying it's bad for other people or anything like that; however, since I have grown up with very few life experiences and living on an island six miles out in the middle of nowhere for these last many years, I have to spread my wings and experience a few things first. At least that is how I am seeing things right now!*

Now, how could I say that to Emile without crushing his spirit and having him hate me in the process? Good question. I needed some more Mom and me time. On second thought, I probably should plan on some Dad and me time as well to get this straight in my head. Their counsel and input meant so very much.

Thank you, Lord, for the extra-most-bestest parents!

The talk with Emile turned out to be a bit of a puzzle for me. I didn't know what had just happened, and I was confused!

He commented, "It seems to just be a case of bad timing between you and me right now. Maybe the little age difference plays a small part in that. That is not a bad thing, but it means we have to go our separate ways for a while until you experience those things that are in your plan. I'll be around. I am not going anywhere."

His comments hit me like a ton of bricks. I decided to leave rather abruptly, still trying to process what I considered to be his carefree response.

I said, "Thanks for meeting, but I have to run. Please pray for me."

He responded, "I definitely will pray."

I decided to share my conversation with Mom to see what she thought about Emile's response.

I said, "Mom, it sounds like he is willing to back off without the least little bit of emotional stress or concern. He thinks we have bad timing, that our age difference is a problem, and that we should go our separate ways! He then nonchalantly and cavalierly says he will be around. Wow! It sounds like he doesn't give a hoot and is being very passive about what I told him! Why am I wasting my time with all of this if that is the way he feels? Huh!"

Mom responded with a slightly different take and stated, "Sweetie, Emile mentioned that he wasn't mad, correct? You also mentioned that he listened intently to your request of him, correct?

With a bit of chagrin, I muttered, "Yes."

Mom continued, "It also sounds like he was willing to be a little patient until you got some life experiences under your belt. I think he might be showing a degree of understanding and compassion, not passivity. Remember, it was you who decided to lower the temperature in the room and not the other way around, right?

I said, "I suppose so."

Mom ended with a flurry, "Let me say it another way to make it a little clearer from my vantage point. He wasn't mad. Check! He listened intently. Check! He showed some understanding and compassion. Check! And he was willing to be patient until you get some life experiences under your belt. Check!

"Perhaps you need to give him a little more credit for the way he handled your request for him to back off? He might have been trying to minimize the age difference and not magnify it. What do you think?"

I responded, "I guess I need to think about it a little more and give it some thoughtful prayer. I might have overreacted a bit. I'm just not sure right now."

15

GETTING AWAY

I T HAD BEEN OVER FIVE MONTHS NOW SINCE I HAD TO POLITELY lower the boom on Emile LaPierre. He seemed to have taken it in stride and had backed off considerably since our last talk. I did appreciate him doing that and living up to his commitment to pray for me. On reflection, I might have wildly misjudged his response during our previous conversation.

On the few occasions when I bumped into him at church, Emile made a point to say that he was praying for me. He was quick, to the point, and then kept moving along so as not to crowd or pressure me. I noticed his approach, and it meant a lot.

It was now approaching summertime in June of 1916, and I was starting to get the same itch my brothers had about getting off the island and setting out on my own. The desire had been bubbling up in my mind for months now, ever since I caught one of my sisters in my bedroom rifling through my things. While I would never blame Reet directly for my obstinacy and desire to get off the island, it was a tipping point that made me realize it was time to say goodbye.

After an exhilarating afternoon of walking around the island and exploring, I went into my room only to find Reet combing through my drawers.

I asked, "Reet, what in the world are you doing? Who gave you permission to be in my room and to go through my personal belongings?"

Reet responded, "Us girls always look in your room as a last resort when we can't find something. I know you don't want us there, but we do it when you are not around so you won't get mad like you are now."

Growing more irritated, I said, "Do you hear yourself? You know I don't want anyone in my private space, but you do it anyway behind my back!"

By this time, I was spitting nails, and Reet knew she was in the wrong. I was trying to keep a level head and correct her in the right spirit, but I was losing this particular battle. My temper was getting the best of me.

She very sheepishly and nervously uttered an apology. "I am so sorry, Mumsy. You are right, and it won't happen again. Please forgive me."

While I immediately forgave her and moved on from the incident, it reinforced the desire festering within my soul. Bottom line, I needed my independence!

I'd had so many cherished and unforgettable memories here on Franklin Island, but I was getting restless, longing for my independence, while understanding that I needed to start growing up a bit in a bunch of different areas. Sometimes I still felt like a little girl, when in reality, I was an eighteen-year-old woman now (almost nineteen), ready to conquer the world in a nice and wholesome kind of way.

I really didn't know why I was so nervous about talking with my parents about my decision to move off the island. I'd already had a dry run and a dress rehearsal with the boys several years back when they were getting ready for their own "big talk" with Mom and Dad. I knew how it had gone for them and assumed it would go the same way for me.

In other words, I would tell them my plan for living with some friends, getting a job, and finding a solid local Christ-preaching church, and they would happily give me their blessing.

What else were they going to say or do? I was almost nineteen years old, had made mostly good decisions, loved the Lord, and had grown up quite a bit over the last three years. All the kids in our family regularly came to me for advice; I was controlling my temper for the most part; Mom greatly relied on my help around the house;

I was constantly thinking about spiritual things during the day; and most surprisingly of all, I could carry on normal conversations with the opposite sex now! I now needed to take the next step for my personal growth as a woman! I needed some independence! What that might look like, *God only knew.*

Surely they would have no qualms about me moving to Portland, Maine, to live with friends and be near my older brothers, would they?

I began by telling them I was going to share an apartment with three other girls who were high school friends from Scarborough. They listened intently with no comments. So far so good!

Next, I said I planned to work in a fish factory down on the waterfront on Commercial Street in Portland. Still no comments, but I noticed Dad's facial expression did start changing a little.

Then I tried to "sell them" on the idea that I was ready to be on my own and could handle what would come my way. I figured the "self-confidence" angle might score me some additional points.

After I was finished, Mom spoke up and asked, "Are there any other considerations or concerns you need to think about with this move?"

Boom! Mom had just lowered the boom! I didn't know how to respond to the question. I knew she must be driving at "something," but I just couldn't put my finger on what that "something" actually was.

The only thing I could come up with was some kind of a safety concern with me being a one-hundred-pound girl, soaking wet and roaming the streets of Portland, Maine.

That had to be it!

Dad had probably bent Mom's ear with the worry that it was not safe in the big city, and I would be putting myself in danger somehow.

So I responded, "If you are worried about my safety, my roommates and I have already agreed that we will go nowhere all alone in the city and will make sure we are always together with at least two of us present."

Bang! That's it and I nailed it! I think I just punched my ticket to Portland, Maine! Yippee!

Nope, not so fast, cowgirl! Hold on to your Conestoga horse buckle!

Mom responded, "No, sweetie, that isn't our concern at all. Your dad and I already assumed you would make those kinds of safety arrangements. We were concerned with several other things. First, your father and I are convinced that Emile LaPierre will follow you to Portland once he finds out you will be leaving Franklin Island and moving there.

I responded, "Mom, I am not even all that interested in Emile LaPierre. Why would he follow me all the way to Portland when I hadn't shown much interest at all and told him to back off?"

With grace and a smile, she continued, "He will follow you to Portland because he is in love with you, Lola."

That is ridiculous, I thought to myself!

Hoping to get some further clarification on the "love angle" from Mom and Dad, I responded, "I told Emile that I needed space to be my own person and have some independence, and he agreed. I am not sure what you mean by 'he loves me?' I have never encouraged anything of the kind, as I purposefully have kept him at a distance!"

Mom continued her dissection of my reasoning: "Second, have you given any consideration at all to the fish factory job you keep speaking about? Are you aware that the Portland waterfront area is crowded with lobstermen and fishermen coming home from long voyages at sea, and some of the women who work at the fish factories during the day double as ladies of the night during the evening hours? Surely you are aware that the Commercial Street area is a bit rough, aren't you, Lola?"

Pow! Mom had just thrown a very hard left cross! Okay, now I was completely on the defensive and didn't know what to say or how to respond.

I now had two choices. I could try to make something up and lie to fit the occasion so I could further my argument to be on my own, or I could be truthful and say I had not considered these three very big items of concern.

I chose the latter and said, "No, I wasn't aware of the problems down on Commercial Street."

My truthful response might have cost me my independence, but I hoped I had grown up enough in the Lord to always be upfront and forthright!

While I made the right decision to be totally honest with them, the Emile "love thing" continued to hit me hard! My mind was now racing around and being tormented by it.

Mom smiled with a compassionate and loving smile and said, "Honey, he backed off because he does love you and doesn't want to chase you off by being too demanding."

I sighed and then muttered the first thing that popped into my head. "I don't know why since I've been very consistent with him about not wanting to get into a serious relationship right now."

After a very long, silent, awkward pause from the back-and-forth discussion between the three of us that seemed like an eternity, Dad very firmly but lovingly said, "How about we meet halfway for about six months?"

My ears instantly perked up since I thought I might be getting an emphatic "no" after Mom firebombed me with all her questions!

I felt like Daisy when her ears perked up after noticing a Mallard Duck falling from the sky or when she got a command from Razor to go and retrieve some other vermin. I was all ears right now!

He continued, "You get to move off the island and be on your own, but your mom and I are satisfied that you are in a situation closer to home where both Emile and your work environment can be sorted out. What do you think about living and working in Friendship? You could take an apartment, find a job, figure out this Emile thing, attend a familiar local church, but still have the counsel of your parents when you want it. It is only for six months, and then if you decide to move to Portland, we will fully support your decision, with the exception of the fish factory job."

Dad smiled and winked after he finished with the "fish factory" comment since he knew I probably would pass on that job now that I know a bit more about the "local clientele."

I immediately thought to myself, *Well, it isn't an outright no, and what they are saying does kind of make sense.* They loved me unconditionally and had my best interests at heart. But the problem was that they wanted it on their terms and not my own. Isn't that what being independent is all about? Shouldn't I be able to make my own decisions right now and do the things I wanted to do?

I responded, "Mom and Dad, I know letting me go out on my own is a very big step for you both. I am just not sure right now that your solution is best. Let me pray about it for a few weeks and get back to you."

The next two weeks were a spiritual wrestling match for me. I now felt what it was like when Jacob wrestled with the angel.

My mind kept coming back to the point of being a spiritually minded adult. Should I demand my independence or submit to the will of my parents?

At the end of the two weeks, I gave them my answer.

I said, "Mom and Dad, I am willing to stay in Friendly as you have suggested, but I just want to make sure you will allow me the independence I need to grow and flourish on my own. I need a lot of space right now."

I could tell they were very relieved.

Those six months would allow me to gain more perspective before jumping headlong into the claws of a big city scenario and within range of an overly persistent suitor! And, if my parents lived up to their end of the bargain, I would gain some much-needed space and independence.

I was also relieved and thankful to God for pricking my spiritual sensibilities and working this all out. Well, at least for now.

The last few weeks had been a whirlwind of hustle and bustle. I spent much time finding the right apartment and searching for just the right employment opportunity in Friendship, Maine. It didn't take me too long to narrow down my list to a perfect little one-room efficiency apartment. It had everything I needed—a small icebox, running water, a sink, a metal tub for bathing, a bed, a small table, and a small combination wood-burning cooking and heating stove.

There were only a couple of problems. First, the toilet was in the middle of a common area I would be sharing with two other tenants! Yuck! Gross!

While the landlord was very kind and hospitable as he showed me around the apartment and described all of its unique features and benefits, he too, apologized for the bathroom situation.

He said, "I understand that sharing a bathroom might not be ideal, but that was partially why I lowered the rent to where it is now. I don't believe you will find a more reasonably priced efficiency apartment in all of Friendship! What do you think?"

I said, "I like the apartment, but I need to get back to you. A few things have to fall in place first before I commit. Thank you for showing me around."

The landlord ended with, "Remember, this is a first-come, first-served opportunity!"

Well, I couldn't beat the price, so I might have to swallow my pride, suck it up, and start getting used to the idea of sharing a bathroom for the next six months. Come to think of it, I had been sharing a toilet with ten other people, including five boys, for a very long time now!

The good news was that the two other tenants were also female— One in her mid-twenties and the other a thirty-something with a three-year-old little boy. I thought I could make this work. When I met with them, they appeared to be reasonable and friendly people.

However, the second issue was a more difficult one to solve. Because the landlord worked on a first-come, first-served basis and I didn't have a job to be able to put down a small percentage of the first month's rent, I could lose out on the apartment. The landlord seemed to be a stickler on the money issue.

I had a couple of options on this front. I could ask my parents for the money or wait until I got a job first and put the money down myself. To ask Mom and Dad would kind of defeat the purpose of being on my own and trying to become more independent. It would force me to go crawling back to my parents on my hands and knees for help so soon after I asked for some personal freedom. I was now caught between an emotional rock and a hard place!

In the end, I decided to wait until I could afford it all on my own. That was the independent thing to do! That was the tough thing to do! I now needed to "pray-in" a job as soon as possible before the apartment was taken by someone else. But first, I needed to figure out where in Friendship I could stay in the meantime.

My first thought went directly to Mr. Jedidiah Grassenpoop (pronounced graws-sen-pop) and his wife, Isabella. They had become such close friends of our family. I was hoping and praying they might let me stay with them *for a spell* until I found a job and had the money needed to put down on that apartment, assuming it was still available.

After I explained my dilemma to Mr. Jed and Isabella, they immediately welcomed me with open arms.

Mrs. Grassenpoop said, "Darling, of course you can stay with us until you sort things out. We would love to have such a wholesome and considerate girl like you keeping us company for a while."

She then turned and looked over to her husband with a great big smile and added, "I get to stare at something very lovely for a while instead of all these putrefied animal heads hanging on the walls smiling at me in an otherwise lovely and well-kept home!"

All three of us shared a very hearty laugh at Mr. Jed's expense!

That was such a relief and so nice to hear. *Thank you, God!*

After Mr. and Mrs. Grassenpoop both agreed in full, I reaffirmed my commitment to them not to stay more than a month. I did not want to burden them or have them think I was trying to take advantage of them. Time was of the essence! I needed to get busy!

The next hurdle was to get a local job to cover my living expenses. For the next few weeks, I searched high and low for an employment opportunity! Nothing! Every business I called on was *full to the brim* and didn't need anyone else on their payroll.

Finally, in week three, I came across an opportunity. Two ladies at our church who worked at the local Friendship Fishing Cannery said their company was looking for some full-time help.

Fishing cannery? Oh, boy! I couldn't wait to tell my parents about this one! But if ladies were saying it was a reputable business, then I would make an independent decision and run with it!

I applied on Thursday afternoon, and before I left the building, the cannery foreman, Mr. Hockenbass, told me to report on Monday at 8 a.m.

At the end of that first week of work with paycheck in hand, I cashed my check and then sprinted (fast-walked) over to the landlord for the one-room apartment that I liked and put the money down to hold it.

I was *a tad little bit* short on the money front, but after some pleading with the landlord, he said, "Well, no one else has shown any interest recently, so it's all yours, missy."

I was so excited that God does answer prayers. I let my family know first and then mentioned my good fortune to everyone and anyone who would listen at church. It was simply the best news! I was going to be an independent woman! Yippee!

After seven weeks on the job, all I could say was, "Fish guts, anyone?"

My daily routine was working in fish guts. I cleaned fish, removed their guts, and got them ready for processing. The "getting them ready for processing" portion of my task involved removing their heads and tails, filleting them into bite-sized chunks, throwing their guts and bony little spines in a big metal bin, and then sending them down a nasty-looking, blood-stained, slimy conveyor belt for the cans.

I had never seen so many Atlantic striped bass in one place in my entire life. It seemed like we got boatloads of these *little buggers* by the minute!

I was always hearing from people who had never worked in a fish cannery or fish market before that Atlantic striped-bass were mild-tasting fish that tasted just like chicken.

"Well, you can keep your diseased chickens! I will never eat another piece of fish the rest of my life now that I know how they are processed! It turns my stomach just to think about eating fish," I said!

It wasn't like I hadn't had any experience in this line of work before. When Razor was home on the island, he kept me up to my "fish eyeballs" in fish guts! Now this ... Yuck!

Mr. Hockenbass was an absolute tyrant when it came to attention to detail and "made no fish bones" about telling anyone and everyone when they made a mistake.

He called people out by name in front of the entire cannery when he saw something he did not like. I got called out two times in my first week, and once in the second week!

I turned three shades of red and was completely embarrassed by his curt and hyper-direct mannerisms on those first three occasions. The two women at my church decided to pull me aside and give me a little advice. Mary Benton and Janice Hightower told me how to navigate Mr. Hockenbass's "tyrannical ocean swells" so I could stay out of his "cross-fins."

I often thought I was living in an alternative reality! When I was at home on Franklin Island, I operated as the "second-Mom," and everyone wanted my advice. At the fish cannery, I was nothing but a necessary evil (hourly employee) who needed to tow the productivity line or else (You're fired!).

I didn't dare to complain to anyone for fear of losing my job and my independence. For now, it was paying the bills, and I was thankful for that!

I had to believe part of God's plan was for me to learn to persevere through the trials and tribulations of the workforce. At this point in my tenure, I was just not sure I would make it. It had been tough sledding.

16

ALL GROWN UP

FIVE MONTHS HAD NOW PASSED AT THE FRIENDSHIP FISH Cannery, and I was surviving my job. Walking that tightrope at work had been an absolutely exhausting chore. It was physically and spiritually demanding and draining! However, it paid my bills and I had a little extra money to spend on myself.

Mom and Dad had been very supportive and had kept a respectful distance, allowing me to grow as a woman and gain some much-needed independence.

We saw each other at church each week, and they even invited me over to the island for a meal on two separate occasions. But for the most part, they had treated me like an adult, as they wanted to see me grow and flourish as much as I did, if not more.

The whole Emile "thing" had taken a little bit of a turn a few months back. I indulged him on a few more "friendly" outings over the last five months, and one of those included a meal with Mrs. LaPierre and Harold. They were a sweet family who had been through a lot but seemed to be coming out on the other side of the divorce. Well, if that was even possible! *God only knows.*

Unfortunately, their father had moved to New Hampshire, married another woman, and had nothing at all to do with the two boys. Emile never spoke of his dad, at least not in my presence. There seemed to be some very bad blood between him and his father, or at the very least, severely hurt feelings and unresolved issues.

I received the news when I saw him at church. Emile's facial expressions weren't as upbeat and cheery as they usually were.

I said, "Emile, everything okay? You don't seem like a happy camper today. What is going on? Who died?"

I asked those questions in jest, trying to be *a tad little bit* playful, not expecting a serious response. In hindsight, I wish I had used another tactic.

With a serious look on his face, Emile responded, "Harold and I lost our jobs at the local construction company. The company fell on very hard times as a result of a competitor coming in and taking a good portion of our customers. The company ended up laying off half of its entire workforce, which included Harold and me, since we are relatively new employees. It is a bit frustrating to our family."

I said, "I am sorry to hear that for your family."

As a result, the LaPierre family had to make a decision and make one very fast. They couldn't afford to keep their home with only one income. Mrs. LaPierre loved her job at the restaurant in Friendship and had been there for a few years now. Her customers also loved her and she made very good tips, but just not enough to afford to keep their home.

It was sad when I learned they had to put their house up for sale and move away so suddenly. I had very mixed emotions. A part of me hated to see Emile and his family leave Friendship. Another part of me was glad not to have the immediate and ongoing pressure of courtship always hanging over my head.

I liked Emile, but he wanted more than I could give right now, and that always made me uncomfortable. Maybe I was just imagining it, but there always seemed to be underlying pressure for me to give more than I was willing to give Emile. Perhaps the distance was God's way of working everything out! I was just not sure either way!

It only took them a month to sell, since it was such an adorable little place that the two boys and Mrs. LaPierre fixed up real nice. They had even added a third bedroom and a big front porch to the original house. The LaPierre boys had a knack for carpentry and construction work.

The LaPierre family ended up moving to Portland, where they thought they could find quick employment, and they were right.

Emile started hauling oil as an independent oil contractor. He had a specific route in Portland that included the Munjoy Hill area and the surrounding community.

From what he told me on the very rare occasions when we saw each other, he had a very successful oil distribution business with a partner of his, Oden Moros (translated raging doom), and his wife, Lilith Ciara-Moros (translated dark night monster).

Emile always seemed to have a pocketful of cash when we went out for coffee and didn't mind flaunting it a little. I believed growing up extremely poor in Canada had made Emile more susceptible to focusing too much on money. Don't get me wrong; I enjoyed an expensive night out with Emile every once in a while! I didn't grow up in that kind of environment, and it was fun. But the constant focus on money made me very uncomfortable. I just didn't like it at all.

Emile working on his oil delivery truck.

Anyhoo, Harold ended up getting a job with Fred Spring Company, which ran an off-street lot and a filling station down on Preble Street in Portland. Mrs. LaPierre had a hard time finding a waitressing job, so she ended up at one of the Fish Markets down on Commercial Street in Portland. I was happy to hear that they had settled in.

Before he left, Emile asked if he could stay in touch with me, and I said I would like that. As it turned out, we left on "semi-good" terms. I was starting to wonder if I should redefine what those "good terms" actually were! I did count him as a good friend.

Emile was starting to grow on me. I was "nowhere" near where he would like me to be in our friendship, but I was becoming more and more attracted to his crazy and outgoing personality, warts and all. Yes, there were plenty of warts, which worried me some. *Tell a lie*! It worried me greatly!

As for my continuing growth journey, I had a very big decision to make in the upcoming month. It would be almost seven entire months since Mom, Dad, and I had our discussion about me moving to Portland.

There was still a desire within my heart to move to Portland and experience more of life; however, I just needed to figure out a way to express my desires to Mom and Dad so I didn't hurt their feelings and it made good overall sense.

The last seven months had been a complete blessing, and I wouldn't have wanted it any other way. Mom and Dad were right; I had some growing up to do and needed to be relatively close to home in the process to work out my spiritual kinks and other "matters" of concern. At the same time, they could see that I needed a little more seasoning with some real-life and real-world experiences.

I believed the last seven months had put me on the right path, and now I was ready to take my next step forward. I was waiting for the perfect opportunity to tell Mom and Dad my plans.

I just needed to pray and make one hundred percent sure the overall timing was right for a move like this! It was a very big decision!

The only monkey-wrench thrown in the works was the rumor going around about my brother Razor. We were told he had fallen in with the wrong crowd in Portland and had been drinking alcohol heavily. The source was very reliable. It was Big Chief's best friend in high school, Nehemiah Treblehorn. We were also being told that he had been spotted on more than one occasion, passed out at a local bar.

I wanted to make sure the rumor was true, so I sent a letter and asked, "Big Chief, are you absolutely 100% sure that the rumors are true about Razor?"

He responded a week later, "Sis, I trust Treble with my life. While he might have been a bit crazy in high school, he was someone I implicitly trusted with the truth. He wouldn't spread and confirm rumors like that if they weren't so."

It was a vice that never reared its ugly head before Razor was on his own and out from under my parents' oversight and tutelage. It was so very disappointing and disheartening to hear about my big brother.

I hoped and prayed that Mom and Dad weren't a little *skittish* about letting me go off on my own to Portland now that Razor was acting out so terribly. Quite frankly, I wouldn't blame them one bit if they were a little *gun-shy* right now. It wouldn't surprise me if they asked me to stick around a few more months while they tried to sort out the Razor mess.

It was the Christmas holiday season once again, and my little village of Friendship, Maine, was gloriously decorated for the Christ season. The Christmas manger was beautifully arranged out in front of our church, a 30-foot-tall Christmas tree was towering over the center of town near city hall, and the pinecone-adorned wreaths with holly, dried orange slices, and ribbons were hanging absolutely everywhere! We also had been blessed with a couple of "dustings" of snow of late, so it looked like we would have another blessed white Christmas!

Okay, okay! So we were in Maine, and I use the term "dustings" disparagingly! You are correct, they were full-blown Nor'easters, and you have anticipated my minimalist initial offering with the word "dustings!" I completely confess to the oversight! We got "slammed" with snow was more like it!

There was a special play tonight at church, and all of my younger brothers and sisters had a part. I was so looking forward to seeing them act out their roles. It was usually *such a hoot* watching them playact!

At about 6:30 p.m., my parents walked into the church to get a front-row seat for a 7:00 p.m. start. With six children in the Christmas play this year, my parents didn't want to miss a thing, so they figured they would get there *a tad bit* early. I finished up my shift at the cannery about 5:30 p.m., ate a quick supper, and then headed over to church.

Dad and Mom immediately came over to catch up on how I was doing and then both gave me very big hugs.

The next words out of my father's mouth were an absolute shocker and sent my jaw to the floor and sent me reeling!

He said, "Hey sweetie, now that you are coming up on seven months living in Friendship, your mother and I have been talking, and we are wondering how we can help you with your move to Portland?"

Say what? They'd beat me to the punch again and had me completely baffled and dumbstruck. I thought our conversation about my pending move might be another nerve-racking event as a result of what was going on with my brother Razor, and I told them as much.

Mom said, "Honey, we have watched you grow up so much in the last six or seven months that your father and I felt we needed to be an encouragement and a blessing to you. We really do see your growth and want to help out anyway we can."

Dad continued, "Sweetie, we have seen how you have managed your apartment, finances, church, and your full-time job with ease. You are being a very good steward with the things God has blessed you with, and we are proud of what you have accomplished! We just want you to know that you have our full support if you still want to head to Southern Maine. Just let us know how we can help."

I didn't have a very good response to their offer of support, other than to say, "Thank you so much for your kind words of support. I need to pray about this for a few weeks and get back to you if that's okay?"

Mom and Dad both acknowledged my request and said that would be fine.

The truth was, while I had been trying to convince myself that the move to Portland was a logical next step in my growth and independence, I had been so busy with work and church that I really hadn't thought through the particulars yet and devised an actual plan. I just didn't want to do anything rash and regret it later.

At the end of two weeks, I gave them my answer. I was direct and to the point and said, "I thank you both for your offer to help move me to Portland, but I'm not quite ready to make the leap for a bunch of different reasons.

"First, I don't think that moving during the winter months is such a good idea. This is one of the worst winters we have had in years, and the forecast is for it to get worse. We have three feet of snow and counting! Second, from what I hear, many businesses cut back on their hiring during this time of year because things slow down a bit. I have been corresponding with Susan Goodlander, and she is telling me that jobs are very hard to find right now. Third, I don't want to get in the middle of Razor's drinking issues right now, as I am sure that he is going to want to see me on occasion. Razor and I always got along super-duper well, and it will kill me to see him like that. It will tear me apart spiritually.

"And lastly, I simply am not as prepared as I need to be prior to running off to another city. I still have a desire to go but just need time to think things through and have a good overall plan. Finding a city, an apartment, roommates, and employment all take much time and planning and shouldn't be done haphazardly. And then there is Emile. I still need a little more time and some space."

Dad smiled and said, "Sweetie, you are all grown up!"

Mom added. "We are so very proud of you!"

17

THE UNEXPECTED

FIVE MONTHS HAD NOW PASSED, AND THE MOVE TO GORHAM, Maine, had gone off without a hitch as a result of the months of planning and preparation. Yes, I did say Gorham! God had a way of changing our lifelong plans when we were not looking!

The more I thought and prayed about the move, the more convinced I became that Portland was not the answer at this point in my life, especially when first starting out.

Gorham was one of those smaller, sleepy little towns with very good access to Portland, without having to live directly in the hustle and bustle of big city life. Mom and Dad were especially happy when I told them of my decision.

I picked the month of June for my departure. It seemed like a good time of year to make such a transition. Warm enough to avoid that stinging and biting cold winter air, but cool enough to allow me to run around town and get done what I needed to get done without becoming an overheated and sweaty mess.

I took the train from Wiscasset to Portland and got a lift from Portland to Gorham. Dad and Mom accompanied me from Friendship to Wiscasset to see me off. I said all my goodbyes to my wonderful brothers and sisters on the Sunday before at church. I was going to miss them. It was *a tad bit* emotional. *Tell another lie,* it was very emotional! It was the great big group hug by my siblings that did me in. The second they gathered around me and started hugging on me, I lost it and couldn't stop crying like a baby!

My oldest brother, Big Chief, was kind enough to meet me at the train station and bring me to my new apartment in Gorham. I decided over the winter to be extra cautious about who I chose as a roommate. Yes, I did say roommate and not roommate(s)!

I decided one roommate was plenty when first starting out. Making sure the people in my immediate circle of influence were high-quality folks was a top priority for me right now. Razor was the living example of falling in with the wrong crowd, and I was not going down that pathway. He surrounded himself with all the wrong people and was reaping what he had sown. I had grown a bit hesitant over time about dealing with a bunch of personalities all at the same time. In light of *Razor's folly*, I went in another direction! Regardless, I had made my decision, and that was final!

As God would see fit, my former preacher man, Pastor Goodlander, had a daughter attending college in the area, and I thought it a very good match. We weren't best buddies or anything like that in high school, but I did have a high regard for her in general. Susan Goodlander was my new roomy. While she was a bit straightlaced and nerdy, I was praying that we would get along.

She was attending the Gorham Normal School, which was known for being an outstanding teacher's college. I was just not the college type. I barely made it through middle school as a result of my non-interest in school when attending that barn-red one-room schoolhouse in Scarborough, Maine. While high school was much better because of my homeschool experience on the island, my interests were still not geared toward attending college. It wasn't because I couldn't handle the classwork in school but because I was both bored stiff and awkward socially. Fortunately, I had come a long way since then on the sociability front! Homeschooling, island adventure, getting a job, and living on your own would help do that for you!

The only thing that had piqued my notice on the Susan Goodlander front was that she was a bit of a pack rat and very messy around the apartment. I was determined to stay one step ahead of her in the neat freak department. I like a clean and neat home and would make sure it stayed that way with or without her help.

I had no sooner got settled into my new apartment when two weeks later I received my first visitor! Yup, you guessed it! It was Emile LaPierre being as persistent as ever. He said all the right words, gave me that big cheeky grin of his, and asked me out on a proper date at one of the local restaurants.

I said yes.... He was still living and working in the Munjoy Hill area of Portland, so it was a little bit of a commute. For now, the distance might be just right.

Our first formal "no strings attached" date had been a lot of fun. He was being a perfect gentleman. Emile started our date off with a bouquet of red roses, opened all the doors for me, and conducted himself in a way that totally impressed me. Perhaps some of the warts had started to disappear. Hmm. I wondered why?

Now, don't get me wrong; he was still as motivated and ambitious as ever and talked way too much about money and living the good life; however, I sensed a different level of maturity about him. And that sense of humor, he was so very funny!

As I had done so many times before with Emile, I decided to lay down the exact ground rules for our dating. I told him I was willing to go out on a date with him once a week.

I thought this would give me the much-needed space to still do my own thing but enjoy his company at the same time. I really did enjoy the time I spent with Emile. He was such a *crazy fool* ... but in a good way!

This dating arrangement continued for about the next six months, and we had a hoot doing everything together. Emile got very creative with our weekly dates and left no stone unturned.

We took long summer walks; had frequent ice cream cone dates; took several auto-boat tours around all the islands in Casco Bay; visited the Portland waterfront sites on two separate occasions; had dinner with his mom a bunch of times; regularly attended church together; and visited the Portland Institute and Public Library for a bit of reading one time.

The walk around Peak's Island was the turning point. We spent the day holding hands, talking, and enjoying one another's company. I even had my very first kiss on Peak's Island! Emile was a perfect gentleman with me.

I began to realize that Emile was a very complex, ambitious, passionate, and highly intelligent man who loved his family.

That last part continued to be a big draw for me personally. All the other aspects of his personality were things I could deal with, work with, or put up with. However, the love of family, or the lack thereof, would be an immediate deal breaker for me. And of course, his relationship with the Lord was a top priority!

For several years now, I had observed Emile with his mother and younger brother Harold. They had been his world and his focus ever since their father bailed out on them.

Emile decided to step up to the plate and become the leader in the family and take care of them both, and it showed. That part of his character was like a magnet to me. It stemmed from my own familial relationships and how important they were.

Well, are you sitting down? The unexpected happened. I began to have a change of heart. I decided to "redefine" our relationship and let Emile know I wanted to see more of him during the week!

I couldn't believe this! The tables had now turned, and I seemed to be the aggressor. Not in a pushy or forward kind of way, but I truly would like to see more of him and spend more quality time with him. I missed Emile during the week, and that was starting to worry and scare me *a tad little bit*! Those warts were still there and would rear their ugly heads every once in a while, so I was being cautiously optimistic in my thinking about Emile and our relationship.

Anyhoo, I was just going to run with it and see what God had planned for me with eyes wide open. I needed to have faith that all things would work together for good but needed to be spiritually discerning with Emile's behavior. I also needed to speak with Mom and Dad and let them know Emile and I were seeing more of one another. I needed my mother's counsel and advice! Oh, and Dad's advice too!

I sent them a letter and asked if they could burn one of their vacation weeks and come down and visit me in Gorham in a few months' time. They thought it a splendid idea, as they missed me and would use it as an opportunity to visit other friends and extended family members over in Scarborough at the same time. Killing two Franklin Island birds with one stone, so to speak. We ended up setting up the last week of August as our planned get-together.

I mentioned to Emile that my entire family was coming down to visit me in August, and he seemed to be very pleased. Actually, he seemed to be over-the-top excited about my family's trip, which I found a bit strange.

Emile started scheming about some of the things we could do while they were here. I just wrote off his enthusiasm as wanting to be a good host while they visited.

I just hoped he would act like himself and not try to be more than he was around my family. My Dad would see anything fake coming a mile away. He didn't like phony.

August rolled around, and we were now in the thick of the summer months in the beautiful State of Maine. It was absolutely breathtaking! The dog days of August had been spectacular!

So far, we had avoided that 90-degree humid Maine weather we typically got in August, and it had been picture-perfect and in the high 70s and low 80s.

Thank you, Lord! I couldn't imagine the summer getting any better than this, or could it?

We picked Mom, Dad, and the kids up at Union Station Railroad Depot in the Libbytown section of Portland. It was such a convenient location since it was a hop, skip, and a marital jump to both Scarborough and Gorham.

The plan was for Emile and me to go with my mom and dad to visit our extended family in Scarborough first before heading up to my apartment in Gorham. It would be a great opportunity for the extended family to meet my boyfriend, Emile.

Boyfriend Emile? I couldn't believe those words had just crossed my lips! Boyfriend, huh! I couldn't believe it!

Had I decided to leave Emile's warts behind and not think about them? Should the focus on money, the braggadocio, and the worldly conversation and behavior still concern me? Should they be deal-breakers? All questions I must reckon with very soon!

It was simply a fantastical day! Great weather, great fellowship, and just the best overall time I'd had since my early days on Franklin Island.

Our next sightseeing adventure with Mom and Dad and family would be this Friday down at the Portland Headlight in Cape Elizabeth.

This was the very first lighthouse ever built in the State of Maine. President George Washington commissioned its go-ahead and construction. The town of Cape Elizabeth did an outstanding job of operating and taking care of this magnificent national treasure.

This was a part of Maine where many of the *high muckety-muck* types liked to buy their vacation homes, and I totally understood why. It was one of the most awe-inspiring and picturesque places in Southern Maine and in all of New England, for that matter. Well, check that. Franklin Island was right up there too!

We were having so much fun walking up and down the trails and venturing out onto the rocky coast of Maine. We could even see a bunch of islands and a military fort-like structure off in the distance. There wasn't a more soothing and tranquil sight than those darling little waves hitting the rocky shore. They were simply hypnotic!

About noon, we decided to take a little tour of the Portland Headlight lighthouse itself and headed down the path to take us there. Emile had been excitable all day long and seemed to be thoroughly enjoying himself. I had never seen him so full of boundless energy. Then again, there was nothing like a beautiful August day on the rocky coast of Maine!

Just as we gathered as a group to stream into the lighthouse, Emile indicated to our entire family that he had something to say.

I thought to myself, *Okay, what is this clown up to now?* You just never knew what joke or what antics he might come up with to get a laugh from everyone and to further lighten the mood.

He then proceeded to get down on one knee before an onlooking crowd that included more than just my family members and asked me to marry him.

His exact words were, "Lola, I have loved you from the first day we met. Will you marry me and spend the rest of your life with me?"

Emile pulled out the ring and waited patiently for my response.

Okay, in a nano-second, I had a thousand and one different thoughts floating around inside my head. What about Mom and Dad? Had he spoken to them? Were they in agreement?

I quickly glanced over at them and received a wink and a nod from Dad and a smile three miles long from my mother. Great, they were on board!

Next, I did a very quick three-hundred-and-sixty-degree examination of my thoughts, feelings, and motives for wanting to get married, if at all. Did I love Emile, and was the timing right? What about his lingering warts?

After a brief pause, I said, "Yes, I will most definitely marry you, Emile, because I love you and you have been very patient with me!"

We embraced to the roar of our onlooking and adoring "fans."

Can you believe it? I was getting married. Now, if that didn't *hit me right upside my head*! This had been a *wicked good day*!

18

A WRETCHED DETOUR

Y WEDDING DAY WAS TWO DAYS AWAY, AND MY MAID OF honor, Madelynn, and I were scurrying frantically around trying to tie up any and all loose ends. There was so much to take care of. Emile was helping out the best he could, but with his oil delivery route and furnace maintenance business, he had been right out straight taking care of customers.

While my sister Mad and I were in many ways polar opposites growing up, I loved her unconditionally, and we had grown much closer as young adults. We relied on each other and confided in one another all the time. And, talk about the perfect personality to plan and pull something like a wedding off, she was our girl!

With all her *fancy-schmancy* taste in clothes and *high muckety-muck* ways, Mad would have this wedding looking absolutely picture perfect!

I could never have pulled it off all on my own in a million years! Mom was also a great sounding board and confidante as well! I could tell she was enjoying the wedding process much more than the rest of us. She was constantly smiling!

All of my sisters would be bridesmaids, and Emile had chosen his brother Harold to be the best man. Emile and I asked all five of my brothers to be groomsmen, and they all agreed, Razor included.

I was very happy that Razor had decided to be there. With all of his problems with liquor the last few years, I honestly wondered if he would skip our wedding so he didn't have to face Mom and Dad. They were on the outs.

I couldn't think of a better event for family unity than a great big fat wedding. We were expecting over two hundred folks on Saturday afternoon! Yikes!

Our wedding day had arrived, and I was stressed. I couldn't get my hair to lie flat, my wedding dress was wrinkly, my shoes were a bit scuffed up, we were behind schedule, and I was an emotional train wreck! Mad and the bridesmaids were doing their best to keep me upbeat and focused! They kept telling me to smile!

... "I do."

That was one of the last things I remembered before the wedding tornado set in. From that point on, Emile and I were "fair game" to anyone and everyone who wanted to get our attention and congratulate us. It was ongoing and endless. We were being ushered from one room to another, depending on who needed a piece of us the most at any particular moment.

Photos, the main meal, cutting the cake, Harold's best man's pep talk, Dad's prayer, my bouquet of flowers, and all the rest of it got gobbled up and forgotten in the whirlwinds and craziness of the day.

Now, *mind you*, it was an absolute blast, but the pace of the wedding and all the *hoity-toity* events had been totally exhausting.

Okay, okay. I know. I should have been enjoying the moment and thanking the Lord for such a blessing. I was truly thankful to God and appreciative of my little sis, Madelynn, for going above and beyond our expectations.

Based on the results, this was obviously right up her alley. What a blessing she was in making our wedding day the very best it could possibly be. *Thank you, Lord, for my little sister!*

Time was soaring by, and it had been almost two years now since Emile and I had tied the knot. We had settled into a nice, quaint little neighborhood with a beautiful home just down the street, a few blocks away from Munjoy Hill.

We were enjoying it tremendously. The location was perfect for Emile to reach his oil customers and for me to reach my part-time job. It also gave us great access to shopping and any nightlife we cared to explore, such as shows, the theater, Beano, *a tad little bit* of dancing, and watching the horses run at the horse track. It was all pretty harmless, really. Well, at least I think it was *since we were not overdoing it....*

Emile's partner in the oil distribution business, Oden Moros, and his wife, Lilith Ciara-Moros, had been spending a lot of time with us the last few months. They were constantly inviting us out to dinner with them and showing us around town!

After dinner, we usually headed out to a show or some other form of entertainment and had a *small glass of wine* with them while we were there. They liked to make these hilarious and outlandish toasts with their liquor, so we joined them with just *a tad little bit* of wine so we were *not being spoiled sports.* I was so impressed with how smart they were and how much fun they seemed to have all the time! They were just loosey-goosey kind of folks!

Emile was making a lot of money right now, and we seemed to be spending it as fast as he made it. The oil business was lucrative and thriving, and with my part-time job, we had way more money than we needed.

We were burning through the oil distribution money like it was water! Emile was always taking out rolls of $50 and $100 bills from his pocket and putting them on his dresser before he went to bed at night.

As a child, I would never have imagined such extravagance. My family was as poor as dirt. I got very used to hand-me-downs, used toys, used books, and all things that were free. Mom and Dad scraped and scrimped just to make ends meet. Dad might have had some coins jingling in his pocket every once in a while, but he certainly wasn't going to bed with $50 and $100 bills on the top of his dresser. Was not happening!

It was a lot of fun going out shopping and not worrying about where the money was coming from. Certainly a huge change from my childhood. We just bought what we wanted and knew Emile would have a great, big fat paycheck at the end of the week. I liked living this kind of lifestyle as long as *we didn't overdo it too much....*

I made my first bet on a horse that weekend. What a rush watching those horses run around the racetrack. I saw a horse walk by me before the races started that looked like a real winner. I even thought that horse might have winked at me, so I asked Emile if he would put *a small bet* on the horse!

It was *just a small $2 bet,* but I shouted, hooted, and hollered that horse to victory and won $10 back because the odds were in my favor. That horse's name was Black Jack. Now, every time Black Jack ran in a race, I made sure Emile put a big fat bet down on him for me just as a novelty. *Nothing too serious, mind you*!

Emile and Oden had also been *betting some money here and there* to try to win a big pot of money at the track. The trifecta and the quinella horse betting seemed to pay out a lot more money than a regular bet, so Emile had started trying his hand at that.

Just last night, Emile hit a big trifecta and brought over $1,000 home. This one winning bet equalized the losses Emile had experienced over the last couple of months. He had been losing big money at the racetrack, and it was starting to worry me some. I wondered about being good stewards of our money. The gambling just didn't seem to support that kind of responsibility.

However, that $1,000 was more money than I made all year long at my part-time job! This betting thing was fun *as long as we didn't lose too much money* in the process....

Friday nights had become "girls' night out" for Lilith and me. We went over to the Catholic Church at the bottom of Munjoy Hill and played Beano. It was a game of chance that involved numbers and a bunch of cards with numbers on them. When the "caller" called out the number and your card became full with your chips, you yelled "Beano" as loud as you could! The louder you yelled, the bigger was your own personal pat on the back!

It was very fast and exciting, and I liked playing multiple cards all at once. If only one person yelled "Beano," then the winnings were much more lucrative. When five or six people yelled "Beano" all at the same time, then the pot was divided up evenly.

While Lilith and I played Beano from 6 p.m. to 11 p.m. on Friday nights, Emile and Oden played cards with a few other business associates of theirs at the same time. They even worked in a few hands of cribbage. Emile loved cribbage! I think he loved it as much as I used to love knitting.

They always had a good time and drank *a few beers* together. *Not too many, but just enough* to have a good time. Lilith and I did the same with a *few glasses of wine*. After I was finished with Beano, Emile came by the Catholic Church to pick me up. We then went out for a quick bite to eat before heading home.

I must confess I had picked up *a tad little bit* of a bad habit lately. I had been doing *a little smoking* while playing Beano. *Not too much, just a little…*

Everyone at the Beano Hall smoked, and I decided to join in with a couple of smokes. I just had two each night of the Marlboro brand while I was playing. *I didn't overdo it or anything like that.* Plus, I used the smokes with the filters on the end that were much better for you.

My parents sent a nice, long newsy letter today telling Emile and me that they missed us and would be coming for a visit in a few weeks. We hadn't seen them in quite a long while! It had been almost seven months! They were spending time in Southern Maine and wanted to get caught up with their oldest daughter and her husband.

Dad had an informal training seminar in Portland, and they thought it would be a great opportunity for the two of them to get away from the island for a few days and visit.

I was looking forward to seeing them and had so much to share with them. The only thing I was not looking forward to was when Mom and Dad asked about how things were going at church. I didn't have a very good answer on that front.

Church for Emile and me had been very sporadic lately as a result of his job. He was always getting called in on Sundays to do this or that at the oil distribution station or furnace maintenance business, which had caused us to miss a lot of church.

If we made it once a month to church, we were lucky. I really did feel bad about not attending church regularly, but Emile had such a great job, and we were making so much money and having such a blast spending it that it was just not the priority it should have been. *Foot loose and fancy free, as they say.*

Mom and Dad met us at our place in Portland, and immediately, I knew something was up! They were being very courteous and cordial with great big hugs, but I could tell something was up with them both. I know my parents!

The four of us sat down at the kitchen table, sipping on a cup of coffee, with some initial small talk and a rundown of how each of my siblings was doing; however, they then proceeded with the "parenting bomb!"

Mom opened the grenade volley with, "Sweetie, your dad and I need to share something with you and Emile and don't want to hurt your feelings. We prayed about it and thought that if we don't say something, we will regret it later as parents. You and Emile are responsible adults, and if it's okay, your dad and I will speak to you like we would any other Christian adults."

We recently heard something from Pastor Goodlander that we wanted to bring to your attention. Susan Goodlander was having some coffee in downtown Portland several weeks back with a friend of hers when she looked out the window of the coffee shop and saw you and Emile coming out of a dance hall with another couple who seemed to be hooting and hollering like they might have had too much to drink."

Mom then locked her "mom eyes" on both Emile and me and asked. "Is this true?"

I simply melted in the moment. My face was flushed with embarrassment. I went into justification and legitimation mode, but deep down, I knew we were behaving in a worldly manner.

Ouch! Our cover was blown! Our sin was finding us out! Emile and I sat silent, not knowing what to say or how to respond.

I was the first to respond and said, "Mom, we went to a dance with another couple and were having some fun, and they had too much to drink and got carried away a little bit. I know you don't think that speaks too well of Emile and me and who we are hanging out with, but it's Emile's business partner, and we are trying to keep up good relations for the sake of the business."

Dad, with a caring tone, added, "Sweetie, we would hate to see you and Emile go down a path you will regret later. We love you both."

Then Mom repeated something she said years ago when Emile and I were first in our "friendly" dating mode. It came rushing back into my memory like it was yesterday and *smacked me upside my head*......hard!

She didn't give me the "remember when I told you so" pitch; she just used the same phrase I had heard many times down through the years with all of us kids.

With a mother's concern, she said, "Your dad and I have confidence that God will lead in your family and that virtue, consistency, and involvement in a local church is the right spiritual path for you and Emile. We love you."

The words virtue, consistency, and involvement keep swirling around in my head and would not leave. What had Emile and I been doing? I was so ashamed! My parents were probably worried we were going down the same path as my brother Razor!

He was a full-fledged alcoholic now who had a very bad reputation around town and was quite the *hooligan*. They probably thought we were in some sort of meltdown mode as well. Spiritually speaking, they might be right!

I was now questioning what kind of reputation Emile and I had around town with all the gambling, drinking, dance halls, Beano, and the smoking we had taken up. All for the all-mighty dollar and the satisfaction of living the good life. This hurt and was a *kick in the pants*!

Mom and Dad would never compare one of their children against another, but with all the heartache they were having with Razor and his alcohol, I knew it must be top of mind for them with their concern for us.

Emile finally spoke up and commented. "Thank you for concern and bringing this to our attention. Lola and I will discuss this in private."

This was Emile's way of reestablishing his position as leader of our immediate family and indicating that the conversation was now between him and his wife.

However, what worried me greatly was the lack of any kind of contrition in his response to them. There wasn't an ounce or even a hint that we might be doing something we shouldn't be doing. Nothing!

There was no "I am sorry" or "we shouldn't be doing this kind of stuff" or "we have taken it too far" or anything of that nature. I immediately knew Emile and I might not exactly be on the same page, and we needed to work through this as husband and wife.

The spiritual angst between Emile and me was palpable right now. It went much deeper than the gambling issue. It spoke to the core of our marriage.

Needless to say, the rest of the afternoon was a bit awkward. Mom and Dad wanted to continue to visit with us to bring some normalcy back into the equation before they departed, while Emile and I were biting at the chomp to have a talk and figure this whole thing out!

They decided to leave about 4:30 p.m., and we were relieved. I loved my parents dearly, but they had just launched a spiritual grenade our way, and we needed to perform some immediate triage.

It wasn't like they were unkind at all when speaking with us, but the content of their "truth-telling" was something Emile and I couldn't avoid and must deal with. We now had "a very big, fat, white elephant" sitting in our front room, and it was not leaving anytime soon!

The conversation between Emile and me didn't go all that well. We spoke with one another from very different perspectives and talked past one another on many occasions.

Emile's perspective came from one of claiming "moderation" in our actions and protecting his business relationships and interests, while mine came from what was now a very "big conscience" of knowing right from wrong. I guess you could say I was tired of touching the very hot stove or, at a minimum, standing way too close!

How in the world would we ever reconcile those two very different perspectives? Emile and I needed to get back to the basics, which meant much-needed prayer. But honestly, the basics included a lot more than just prayer. It included a complete lifestyle change. We had gotten off track and needed to regroup and reprioritize first principles and the Word of God.

I started reprioritizing spiritual things in my life and made sure I was in church whether Emile could make it or not. I also started declining invitations from the Moros family. Emile wasn't too happy with that at first but began to understand over time.

Emile was such a hard worker, and I knew he wanted to be a great business success and provide for our family, but we needed to sit down and "count the cost" of the direction we were headed in.

Over the next year, we had our ups and downs. I had been praying about both our business attachment and our personal association with the Moros family. The bottom line was that they were just not a very good influence on Emile and me, regardless of the business connection. I had been trying to be supportive of Emile, but I was now making it very clear to him when lines were being crossed.

Emile and I were committed to our marriage even during these very dark and difficult times.

Beyond the obvious spiritual shortfalls with our worldly behavior, we seemed to be throwing a lot of good money after bad with our gambling, and we were not being very good stewards. For the first time since we had been married, we lacked money for a monthly bill.

Emile commented, "We have an oil truck payment coming up, and we are a little short this month. I am going to have to work some extra-long hours the next few weeks."

With a bewildered look, I asked, "Has the business been slowing down lately? Have you lost any customers? Why the shortfall?"

When Emile didn't respond and walked out the door to our home, I immediately understood the situation. His gambling had put us in a temporary hole we needed to dig ourselves out of. This was now getting out of hand, and I was overwhelmed with outright anxiety and concern. Was his gambling now getting totally out of control?

19

CHRIST ANEW

WHAT A DREADFUL AND WRETCHED DETOUR WE HAD TAKEN with our lives. My parents were very generous in their assessment and obvious understatement of their concern about where we were headed as husband and wife. We were experiencing some very dry bones in our marriage right now, and there was much spiritual consternation. I knew my parents were disappointed with our behavior, and that concerned me greatly because I knew they were right. I was too self-aware to allow my sin to go unnoticed!

I also knew they were lifting us up in much-needed prayer as a result of the decisions Emile and I must make in the future, one way or another.

Then, a little ray of hope and some glorious light. About five months later, Emile came home one night from work and asked me a very simple and straightforward question that spoke mountains!

We were sitting down eating supper together, getting caught up on the day, when he asked me, "Lola, what do you think of selling our half of the oil business and moving out to the country?"

Say what? I was so overjoyed that I *bout fell over backwards* in my chair!

I worked very hard at composing my enthusiasm and replied, "I think that is a very good idea, Emile."

My reply was short and sweet, "trying" not to show one morsel of exaggerated emotion. I remained calm and didn't start acting all crazy and jumping for joy right in front of him.

I wanted to make sure he was making decisions for our family that were pleasing to the Lord and not just pleasing to me to keep me happy.

You know that old saying, "A happy wife is a happy life." I was walking a very fine line, and I needed to use much godly wisdom as his wife.

Emile confessed that he was not happy with the direction our lives had taken since we had gotten married and that he wanted to be a much better husband. He expressed his desire to be more unified as husband and wife in decision-making and getting away from our worldly behavior. I sensed a genuine concern from Emile for spiritual things that I had never seen before.

I then asked, "Where do you think a good place in the country would be for us to live and start out fresh?"

Emile replied, "I am not quite sure of the exact location just yet, but I think that God might be leading us to more of a rural setting away from the city at this point in our lives." With disappointment and a bit of chagrin on his face, he added, "There are just too many temptations and pulls with big city life, and I think we need a change right now. I admit, I am struggling!"

I replied, "I agree with your point about city life, and I think we need to replace all that stuff with something much better. Emile, wherever we end up settling, we should make it a priority to find a good church and use that as our anchor and starting point."

Emile nodded in agreement.

I couldn't help it, but tears started to well up in my eyes and were flowing down my cheeks uncontrollably. I was now sobbing like a baby.

Emile asked, "Lola, is everything okay? Why are you crying like this? I thought that you would be happy?"

I responded, "Prayers are being answered, and I am overjoyed at your decision to move out of the city. I just feel like God is moving in our family and wants to write a new chapter in our lives. There is no pain or disappointment in my tears. My crying is pure joy.

He replied, "I am so sorry for putting you through all of this."

That began our diligent search for a new home and the hope of a brighter Christ-filled tomorrow. We looked at a bunch of beautiful small country towns, including Standish, Cornish, Steep Falls, Sebago Lake, Windham, Buxton, Hollis, and more, but the one town we kept coming back to over and over again was Limington, Maine.

There was a great little church "up the road a piece" from the little league field on the right in Limington with a Pastor who preached God's Word and members who were as *friendly as all git-out!*

They had three services on Sunday, one during the week, and were always putting on sweet fellowship opportunities from time to time. Pastor John Nathan Hunter was a wonderful young *preacher man* who knew his Bible inside and out. The deacons were extra friendly and made us feel right at home when we visited the church.

Emile and I had taken a special liking to one particular deacon named Larry Wilcox. He was a long-time teacher at the middle school over in West Buxton, Maine. He was retired now but still very active at church and in the community.

After getting to know Mr. Wilcox *a tab bit* over a nice meal that he and his wife invited us to, it seemed like Mr. Wilcox knew everyone in the entire State of Maine. He was a very well-connected man!

We also found this great little farmhouse up on the top of the Hump Back Road in Limington that we could make work just fine. With Emile's construction background, he would have that place all fixed up and ready to go "faster than you could say lickety-split!"

It came with about twenty acres of land, which was nice for long walks, fishing, and any hunting that Emile might try. There was also a pole line up the road a piece with lots of deer. He liked to hunt and was a very good shot. No surprise there since he was good at most things he put his mind to. It even had a nice-sized stream flowing through the middle of the acreage that was chock full of rainbow trout and some brownies mixed in.

We were both very excited about moving from a tiny house lot with lots of neighbors piled on top of us to a large parcel of land with the freedom to roam. We were hoping that freedom included much spiritual rest as well. The potential spiritual solitude was so very alluring!

The only downside we noticed about the property was the small junkyard situated about halfway between the farmhouse and our neighbors. Emile thought he could get rid of most of the junk at a local scrapyard and even make a bit of money at the same time from the metal and copper wire that he noticed.

I knew we had finally made it to the other side when Emile made an analogy with a fun little spiritual quip.

He said, "Lola, this junkyard that I plan on cleaning up on our property is much like the spiritual junkyard that I had to clean up in my own life. Most of it needs to be gone in a hurry, but there are still some small nuggets mixed in that God can use and ones that we can benefit from."

I smiled and replied, "Emile, you are a wonderful husband with many outstanding qualities. I agree that we both need to learn to let God use those little nuggets for His glory."

Speaking of our new neighbors, we met the Ball family last week, and they seemed like very friendly people. They lived just up the street, about a quarter mile partway up the hill. One thing for sure was that they loved their pet Chihuahuas! Last count, Emile and I thought they might have twelve of those *little buggers* running around! They sure were fearsome little critters for their size! There were lots of very nice children and lots of Chihuahuas in that family!

This might sound silly, but I was really looking forward to getting back to my knitting. With all the late nights and weekends with Lilith over the last few years, I just hadn't had much time for my knitting passion! Can you believe that? I suppose I should call it my knitting obsession, really. I needed to get back on the knitting train track! I found it to be a place of great spiritual joy, solitude, and comfort. It had always been a time for spiritual reflection that I had greatly missed.

The tough part of this whole relocation thing was when Emile had to have the heart-to-heart conversation with Oden and Lilith and tell them about selling our half of the business. We had the option to sell it to a third party or possibly let them buy us out.

I didn't anticipate it would be a very pleasant conversation in the least. Especially, in light of the way they had been giving us the proverbial cold shoulder lately.

Emile asked me to come along with him when speaking with the Moros family about our plans to move to Limington and sell our half of the business. He asked them if they would meet us at the downtown oil distribution business office, and they agreed.

We thought it best to keep it all business, and the office location would be the appropriate place to break the news to them.

As soon as Emile started giving them the general direction and concept of our decision, they immediately went into action and started fussing, complaining, and *throwing a big, giant hissy fit*. They were not happy campers right now!

Oden stated emphatically, "You can't do that … we have an agreement! You agreed that if either one of us leaves the business, then the other takes over with no strings attached!"

Lilith then started in with her tirade and quipped, "All you two wanted to do was use us to make a lot of money and take advantage of our generosity. I told Oden that I smelled a couple of rats several months back."

In a firm but professional voice, Emile replied, "Now wait a minute, we've had a very successful business partnership over the last several years, and we count you two as friends. We have just made a decision to go in a different direction and want to move out of the city. Lola and I just feel that it's best for our marriage if we leave the city and focus more on our family and spiritually minded things. And, as far as any agreement was concerned regarding the business, I never agreed to such terms."

Lilith, who started displaying increased levels of anger and resentment, sarcastically shouted, "Oh, so you two are all high and mighty now that you have sucked this business dry and stuffed your pockets with cold-hard cash!"

Emile closed his eyes for a moment and shook his head in disappointment, disbelief, and disgust.

Then Oden jumped back in with a condescending and threatening retort, "I guess we will just see you in court, now, won't we?"

With that last comment, Emile and I looked at each other and knew it was time to leave. We wanted to have good testimonies on the way out, both on the business front and the personal relationship front.

Emile said, "Sorry to bother you, and thank you for your time. I appreciated the business partnership and sorry that it had to end this way."

Emile was purposefully taking the high road to avoid getting into any kind of "tit-for-tat" shouting match or anything that remotely resembled one. I was proud of the way my husband handled himself.

It was almost like God had allowed that situation to play out the way it did so we could make a clean break from the "entanglements" of the past without any hesitation or regret and without looking back.

In a sense, Oden and Lilith confirmed what we knew all along in our hearts. They were not very nice people, and we had no business whatsoever being involved with them. We should have known better, but greed and lust "played us like a fiddle!"

The lawsuit that Oden threatened us with initially went forward and weighed heavily on Emile and me. It would be difficult to cut the ties to our former life when so much of our life savings was invested in the company. I honestly thought we had moved on from our worldly desires and behavior but were anxious to cut all financial ties to the business. Until this was resolved, we were suspended in a state of not knowing whether our finances and savings would be wiped out or not. We believed that God would sort this mess out.

The trial dragged on for almost an entire year!

There was much procedural maneuvering, endless stops and starts, and continued legal parsing of words that finally came to a conclusion. We waited for the judge's decision with bated breath.

When the day of judgment finally came, Emile and I had knots in our stomachs and were *on pins and needles*. We had faith in the outcome either way, but the courtroom setting made us very uncomfortable. I felt stress just sitting there.

Oden and his attorneys tried to argue that there was some sort of "verbal contract" between Emile and Oden that seemed absolutely ridiculous to Emile and me. Unfortunately, our opinions were not legal opinions but only personal ones. It was now up to the judge.

In the judge's final declaration in the case, he stated, "I find it very difficult to believe that Mr. Emile LaPierre poured his life into this oil distribution business for almost three and a half years working 60-to-70-hour work weeks only to leave the business and turn over 100 percent of its value to his partner without equal remuneration. That does not sound like a businessman to me but a half-wit. Claim denied."

We were so overjoyed that we could now move forward and sell our half of the business to someone other than Oden and Lilith. As it turned out, they couldn't afford to buy our half of the business anyway because of how they had squandered away all of their money and destroyed their personal finances.

I honestly believed that God was blessing our decision to move to the countryside and reestablish the importance of Jesus Christ as our number one priority. Emile and I now realized that anything outside of the Bible was just a lot of worthless noise meant to distract us from our real mission in life to spread the gospel message and to please God with our daily walk.

Now, I won't lie to you. Some of the bad habits and vices we had developed took quite a while to completely ditch and get rid of, but we worked on them diligently. The vice that caught us both by surprise was the smoking. It gave us both fits. We both stopped and started more than a dozen times, and it bothered us greatly. Our physical addiction to cigarettes seemed to be more than we could overcome.

Our addiction to "the smokes" continued on for another two years before we finally broke down and asked our pastor for help. Emile and I both knew that the addiction was spiritual, and we needed to have a deeper and abiding faith to kick our bad habits.

Emile was the first to let go of the cigarettes, and I followed after that. I had a few other setbacks down the road but eventually kicked the bad habit for good! *Thank you, Lord!*

Yes, we were making steady progress toward becoming much better versions of our Christ-honoring selves. Emile and I both desired to hear those glorious words, "Well done, thou good and faithful servant."

The few years of our marriage had been filled with blessings from the Lord. I just couldn't express in words how thankful I was for our return to "Christ anew!"

Things were chugging along wonderfully. We loved our church family, Emile's new machinist job had been terrific, and I loved staying home and taking care of things around. And, yes, I was knitting up a "tidal storm!"

Then the unexpected happened! Another special blessing from the Lord ... or two!

20

TWO LITTLE BUNDLES

I HAD BEEN FEELING A LITTLE UNDER THE WEATHER THESE LAST FEW weeks. It was kind of weird. The common, everyday, ordinary smells all had me running for the latrine. Over the last few days, I had been bending over the toilet on a consistent basis and had been *a tad bit* of an emotional train wreck.

I thought it might be my hay fever allergies back again. They always gave me *a tad little bit* of a sickly feeling this time of year. When I lived on Franklin Island with my family, for whatever reason, the allergies disappeared. I supposed it was that clean and salty fresh air!

Anyhoo, I couldn't wait to get over whatever it was that I had.

Check that. I hoped I NEVER got over what I had! Emile and I now believed we had just received the most miraculous gift! We were going to have a baby! At least that was what I thought was going on with me and my body right now.

I was going down to schedule a doctor's appointment with the town doc today just to make sure. This was absolutely the *extra-most-bestest* news! We had been looking forward to starting our family for a long while now.

For whatever reason, the timing had not been right before. If I had to guess, it was the Lord's way of protecting us.

That *highfalutin* lifestyle we were leading back then wasn't conducive to good quality family living. I was so stressed back then with how things were going in our marriage relationship that it was likely impacting my ability to conceive.

All I knew was that I was praying it was true that we were going to have a baby! We would know in a couple of days!

Well, it just so happened that when I arrived at the doctor's office to schedule the appointment, the receptionist said they just had a cancellation and asked if I would like to see Dr. Hopeling right away!

I replied with a most excitable and enthusiastic, "Yes, please!"

The doctor's office was the last place I generally wanted to hang out. It embarrassed me greatly, and I absolutely hated any kind of doctor's visits. They were the most humiliating experiences in the world, and this one was no different. I just continued to focus on the general outcome and not the visit itself. I stayed steadfast in my prayers to God that Emile and I were going to have a baby!

As usual, Emile was patiently waiting for me outside, pacing back and forth in the waiting room full of eager anticipation. He got very amped up anytime he was in a waiting room.

... Confirmed!

Thank you, dear God! I walked out of that doctor's office with the biggest smile on my face, and Emile instantly knew the good news and gave me a great big kiss and a hug!

As I left the doctor's office, I was seriously planning a little joke in my head about acting all disappointed for not being pregnant and telling Emile it was just my allergies back again.

Best laid plans. I just couldn't wipe that great big smile off my face in order to pull it off. I was beaming with joy!

Now to get word to Mom, Dad, and Mrs. LaPierre! We decided that the quickest way to get word to the Clinch clan was to make a telephone call to the Town of Friendship, Maine, and leave word there with Mr. Jed. He would be overjoyed to carry the message to Franklin Island!

We didn't have a phone in our house, and with Mom and Dad still living on the island, they didn't have a phone either. The town of Limington was more than happy to allow us to use their phone to make the call. The officials at the town hall were so happy to hear about our good news!

We also decided to drive immediately to downtown Portland to share the good news with my mother-in-law. She was going to be over-the-moon happy for us. I couldn't wait to see the look on her face.

Even though she was at work down at the fish factory, we took a chance and asked the factory foreman if it would be okay to quickly let her know about the baby. He happily approved and told us to go ahead!

Bad decision! Very, very bad decision! As soon as I got halfway out onto the fish factory floor, that disgusting fish guts smell made me very sick to my stomach. It wasn't just a little nausea but a full-blown volcano kind of sickness. I ran to the ladies' restroom as fast as I could and got very acquainted with the facilities ... shall we say.

The flashbacks I was now having about the Friendship Fish Cannery and "fish-guts" weren't helping matters either!

We heard back from my parents in a letter five days later, congratulating us on the upcoming birth of our very first child. Beyond expressing their enthusiasm and joy for our news and their very first grandchild, their return post was rather a newsy letter, getting us briefly caught up with the general "goings-on" on the island. Mom said she and Dad would give us the full details when they arrived. It was good to hear from them. So much was happening there on Franklin Island and with our extended family.

Albert was now taking high school-level courses, and he was only in middle school. Madelynn had taken over as second-Mom, much to my amazement and excitement. Hocker got a job as an assistant salesman at the hardware store in Friendship. Johnny Boy got himself into a bit of a "pickle" with the rowboat. Reet met a nice young man at church. And Jo-Jo was being as much of a busybody as ever!

The next six months had been a combination of good days and bad days when it came to my health. All I could say was that this baby was very, very big, and I would be completely shocked if it was not a strapping baby boy. There was no way this could be a girl.

How could it be? I was only one hundred pounds soaking wet! I was huge! I was very huge!

I was right! Clifford K. LaPierre was a ten-pound and eleven-ounce baby boy! What a cutie! Emile was overjoyed with the news of the birth of our son. He waited very patiently for over nine hours as he sat outside our bedroom door, pacing back and forth. The doctor made it in plenty of time to deliver the baby in our home.

With love and a smile, I told Emile, "You have been waiting patiently for me my entire life, baby included!"

The next few years were some of the best times of our lives. "Cliff" was growing like weeds and was a healthy baby boy following his father around everywhere he went. He was such a little "tag-along" with his dad that it was adorable to watch.

However, I was the real fortunate one here. I got to spend all day long with this *little whipper-snapper*! It was such a blessing to watch his every new move and hear his fresh and adorable new sounds. I would not call them words quite yet, but he sure was getting close! I thought he was a child prodigy! I must admit, I was completely smitten!

Well, most of the time. I was still getting used to all the poop, pee, puke, and nonstop crying. It had been quite a challenge juggling the demands of this precious little one, taking care of our home, and trying to be the best wife possible! It was a herculean challenge that took some getting used to. Just when I thought Emile's meal would be on time, our son Cliff had an entirely different idea. It could be *as frustrating as all git-out*!

Two years later, we had our second little bundle of joy! Such a wonderful blessing! Carolyn J. LaPierre was born in the wee morning hours to the delight of her mother and father. However, our precious little sweetheart was having a bit of a rough go of it. For whatever reason, she couldn't keep anything down, and the doctor was a bit concerned that she wasn't getting the nourishment she needed to stay healthy.

It had been three days now, and baby "Carol" was still having trouble. We were very concerned and panic-stricken! She was getting more yellow-looking by the day, and we expected that she might have full-blown yellow jaundice. We were in a constant state of prayer for her health. To make matters worse, I was experiencing *a tad little bit* of post-partum depression, which was not helping matters. I couldn't stop balling my eyeballs out at every turn, and both Emile and the doctor were worried.

At our immediate request, the doctor came back out to our home and did another complete and thorough physical examination and said he now believed the baby had a cleft palate and would need surgery when she got a little older.

For now, the doctor mentioned that we'd have to purchase a special kind of bottle for her to drink from. It would help bypass and navigate around the palate area that hadn't completely fused yet. He said it wasn't life-threatening as long as we followed his instructions and the baby got the nourishment she needed.

While we were heartbroken for our little girl, knowing that she faced upcoming surgeries, we were overjoyed and relieved when we learned that it would not be a life-threatening situation as long as we followed the doctor's orders.

Whew! Thank you, dear God, for protecting our little baby girl. Emile and I both expressed such a deep sigh of relief, with many tears flowing down our cheeks with thankfulness.

It was now three years later, and we had so much to be thankful for. Life was unfolding before our very eyes, and every day God was blessing our decision to follow Him.

Now, don't get me wrong, life wasn't always *easy-peasy* or anything like that, but Emile and I knew deep down in our hearts that we had made the right decision when we decided to return to our Lord and Savior Jesus Christ in earnest!

Wait … the best was just ahead and *down the road a piece*!

This is Emile and me with our two precious children, Carol and Cliff.

Epilogue

THE LEGACY CONTINUES

I FEEL COMPELLED AND OVERJOYED AT THE OPPORTUNITY TO SHARE how our family has been doing and the growth we had seen and experienced over these many, many years and decades. I love you all so very much!

Our handsome son **Clifford** went on to have a very successful law enforcement and public service career. He married his high school sweetheart, Jean Marie King, and they had five children of their own. Their names were Michael, Lucinda, Sally Anne, Stewart, and Mary.

Our beautiful daughter **Carol** also had a very successful manufacturing career and worked for a number of years with several different shoe companies before starting a family with her husband, Donald F. Morse. She married her first love, and they had four boys together. Their names were Daniel III, Richard, Tyler, and David.

My Mom and Dad, **Mr. and Mrs. Albert J. Clinch**, decided to leave Franklin Island in June of 1918, not long after Emile and I had our first child. They absolutely loved it there and cherished all of their fantastical memories. What motivated them to move was that they loved their family more than the beauty of the island. They could not imagine being away from their children and grandchildren for long periods of time. It wasn't in their personalities to stay away for long.

They ended up settling down in a small five-room farmhouse in Scarborough, Maine, off the beaten path from US Route One. Dad loved his Golden Retriever, which was the great-great-grandson of our beloved Daisy. Dad went back to work at a local machine shop for a spell while Mom stayed home knitting up a storm! Go figure!

This is a picture of Mom and Dad (Mr. and Mrs. Albert J Clinch) in their late eighties, a few years before they got promoted to heaven. Daisy's great-great-grandson is crouched at their feet.

Teddy (Big Chief) went on to a very successful career with the AFL-CIO Union and lived out his dream of having influence and being well-known. He ended up marrying a very patient woman named Edith. They had two boys together.

Toward the latter part of his life, after his wife passed away, Big Chief went to live on an Indian reservation. Yup, that's the absolute honest truth! He got to be the center of attention after all!

Willie (Razor) continued to explore his three primary passions in life. Hunting, fishing, and drinking were his priorities, and not in that specific order. I loved my brother Razor; he had a good heart.

He would always light up when we saw each other from time to time.

Emile and I led very full and blessed lives and passed away at ripe old ages when God called us home at the appointed time. We bounced around the Greater Portland area later in life and even purchased a bright purple, gaudy-looking house in Gorham that Emile painted and fixed up nice. However, we were forever drawn back to Limington, Maine!

In our senior citizen years, we even rented a small home in Limington next to the cemetery where we would eventually be buried. Yes, Emile and I were laid to rest in the everlasting arms of our Savior at a beautiful country cemetery in Limington, Maine!

Madelynn (Mad) ended up marrying an architect and lived out her childhood dreams of enjoying the finer things in life. Oh, by the way, we never let her forget about those two *lobstas* that she sucked down the hatch with butter streaming down her face when she was a kid. And I mean sucked down!

Peter (Hocker) went on to be a successful entrepreneur, starting a bunch of small business ventures. He even enticed Emile and me to partner in a few of them.

We co-owned and operated a restaurant in Gorham right by the Four-Corners and then started a little five-and-dime store in Portland not far from the post office.

Hocker hit the jackpot when he married his wife, Ruthie. She was my *extra-most-bestest* friend and confidante. Ruthie had a very successful career at the City Clerk's Office in Portland.

If the truth be known, I think she helped fund most of Hocker's business ventures! Oops, I didn't just say that, did I?

Rita (Reet) married a missionary to Nova Scotia. She met him when they were young while attending the Friendship Baptist Church together. As God would have it, they reconnected years later at a church function. They had six beautiful children.

Jonathan (Johnny Boy) enjoyed life to the fullest, always ready to conquer his fears. As the resident daredevil and adventurer extraordinaire growing up on Franklin Island, he too, went on to have a successful business career and was an outstanding family man. He and his beautiful wife, Dorothy, had one child.

JoAnne (Jo-Jo) had a bit of a rough go of it with her relationships with the opposite sex. She had been married and divorced twice and had now decided that being single was the best course for her. Her loud, obnoxious, and demanding ways eventually smoothed out "just enough" for her to become the boss-lady at a local steel manufacturing plant.

The guys at the plant learned to respect the authority of their boss-lady. At least, that was what I was told. I loved my little sis in spite of her overactive personality.

Albert (Al) took his highly functioning brain to a professorship position at the Gorham Normal School, which was now the University of Southern Maine. Those early "primer" books of his definitely had their impact. Albert never settled down and married. He dated many women over the years but was more interested in books and teaching than he was in long-term relationships.

Harold (Emile's brother) settled down in Freeport, Maine. Remember when I mentioned that Mr. L.L. Bean would be repaid many times over for his generosity in ways we couldn't have imagined?

Well, it just so happened (fact) that six LaPierre family members on Harold's side of the family worked at L.L. Bean for decades, which included multiple generations! How was that for coincidence and a return on your Bean Boot investment? Seriously, though, it was pure God-ordained fate! And that "is the rest of the story!"

Jedidiah and Isabella Grassenpoop (pronounced graws-sen-pop) had a very successful and leisurely retirement and were life-long friends of the Clinch family. They operated their "auto-boat" business for over twenty years and eventually sold it for a tidy little sum! To his dying days, he would exclaim, "It's pronounced graws-sen-pop, without the 'grass' and without the 'poop!'"

Hammer-Roy (hemorrhoid) continued their Conestoga wagon service right up until the end of their lives. They made them "some clams" here and there until they finally gave up and declared, "Dat dare new mobile put Roy and me plumb out to pasture!"

Evidently, the game-changing automobile forced them into retirement! At least that was what Mom and Dad thought they said. Hee-hee!

Oden Moros and his wife, **Lilith Ciara-Moros,** ended up having a very rough time of it during the rest of their lives. To say that I saved the worst for last would be the understatement of the century. While I did not wish evil on anyone, it only took a grain of common sense to connect the dots and see where this couple ended up.

Within a year of Emile and me breaking off the relationship, they filed for bankruptcy. Not long after the oil distribution business lawsuit debacle, Lilith filed for divorce from Oden and went on to have a few more unsuccessful marriages. At the end of her life, Lilith was considered a "semi-functioning alcoholic."

Things didn't go all that well for Oden either. He went through a couple of failed business ventures, became a recluse as a result of severe depression, and subsequently ended his own life.

All the fun and games were simply not worth the price of oil!

AFTERWORD

MY PRAYER FOR THIS BOOK IS SIMPLE—THAT IT WILL POINT TO Jesus Christ along with His love, mercy, and grace!

Intellectually, sometimes it's so very difficult for human beings to fathom the depth and breadth of the essence of God—His character; His mercy, love, and judgment; and His revelatory plan found in Scripture for all of mankind to see and to embrace.

The ultimate paradox in God's Word is this ... The more I study, the more I realize the totality of the "known-unknowns" of the Bible as a result of my limited knowledge and sin, which drives me desperately to seek God, His wisdom, and His perfect will for my life again, again, and again!

That God is in control and takes care of His own is one of the underlying messages in this book.

May God bless your individual journeys. I pray that both His common grace (the blessings experienced by all of humanity) and his saving grace (the blessings experienced by those who have a personal and eternal relationship with Him) will envelop and ravish your hearts, minds, and souls.

We accept Jesus Christ by faith as a result of His miraculous and selfless gift on the cross, and we live out our individual blessings here on earth with that same faith-based understanding!

For me and my house, we prefer to be full-to-the-brim with the love and care of a Creator-God, even though we realize our deeply flawed sin natures and struggles with the old man within. We were not perfect ... just yet!

To God be the Glory! Amen.

ADDENDUM

This is me (Lola-Mumsy-Nana) with my grandson Michael James when he was 18 years old. (Family Photo)

This photo is an artist's initial prototype in the early 1800s of what the Franklin Island Lighthouse could potentially look like. (National Archives)

This was the accepted architect's drawing in 1822 of the forthcoming lighthouse, first built on Franklin Island. (National Archives)

A modern-day aerial view that depicts Franklin Island's rugged coastline, the general area of the first mooring, and all of nature's God-given beauty! Oh, and those absolutely gorgeous spruce trees! (Public Domain)

My favorite modern-day era photograph of the Franklin Island lighthouse. I could simply imagine this same location back in 1913 with the Clinch family children soaking it all in, running around, and exploring God's creation! (Courtesy of a paid Commercial Licensing Photo – Photo by Jeremy D' Entremont)

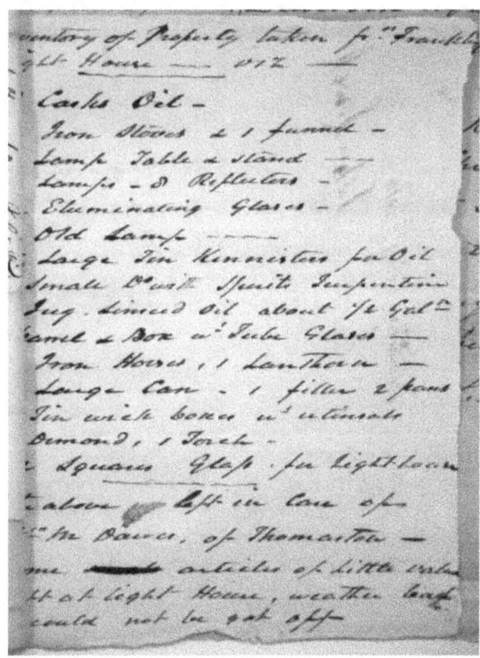

This is a letter of inventory provided by the lighthouse keeper on Franklin Island back in the early 1800s. The very scant listings say it all about the times. (National Archives)

A letter from the Franklin Island lighthouse keeper in 1813. He was requesting his pay from the Collector's Office. (National Archives)

A very old and faint photo of Franklin Island in the early to mid-1800s. Notice the four individuals in the frame. (National Archives)

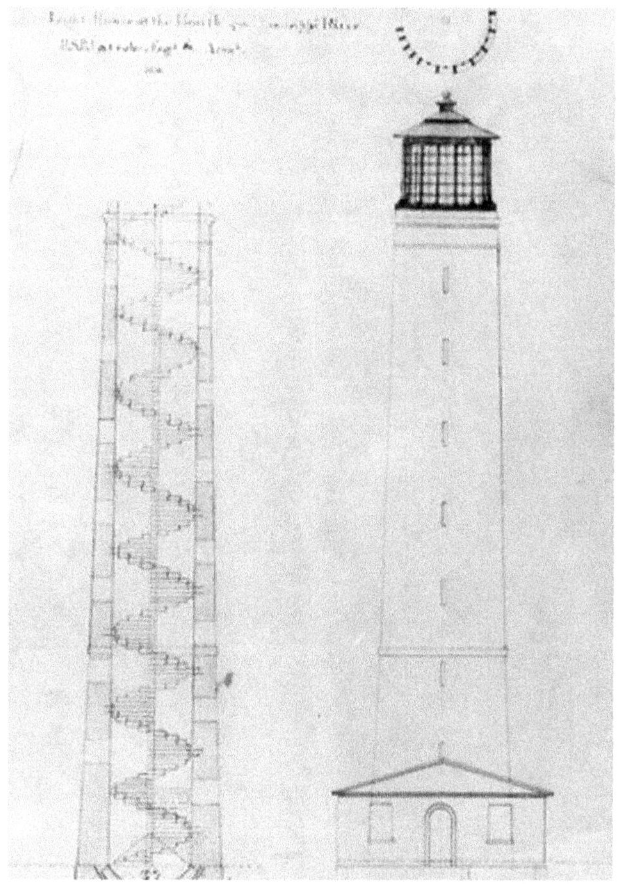

A drawing from the U.S. Coast Guard of the Franklin Island Lighthouse.
(Courtesy U.S. Coast Guard)

AUTHOR'S OTHER LITERARY WORKS

The Christian Leader's Worldview
   This is a framework for successful leadership and living.

God's Gift of Imagination
   It challenges the reader to think outside the box through varying Christian essay perspectives.

The Goldmine
   Operating in a secular world while claiming the workplace for Christ.

A Patriot Manifesto: Convergence in South Carolina Politics
   Setting the record straight by aligning our passion with first principles (Our God-given purpose).

The Elephant Brief
   Documenting the religiopolitical realities of American politics with decisions coming from the U.S. Supreme Court.

A Covenant
   Exploring Christian civic responsibility with a plan for the "Reclamation of Independence" for our beloved America.

COMING SOON...

THE COMPANION TO THIS BOOK IS TAKING SHAPE AND WILL BE out by the end of 2026. The main character of the upcoming book is someone who fought against all odds and won.

The life of the protagonist should never have happened and unfolded the way it did, but God had a better plan altogether, and that plan ultimately impacted hundreds, if not thousands, of believers for the cause of Christ!

ABOUT THE AUTHOR

Michael James LaPierre

As a citizen of the beautiful State of Maine for almost thirty years, I wanted to contribute to the fullness and completeness and let folks know what it's like to be a born and raised full-blooded Mainer who loves the Lord.

My God-given life experiences have been numerous, which means I am getting a little older now and entering the last quarter of my existence here on earth.

I was a Brown University graduate (double-major, Political Science and Business); professional baseball player (minor leagues); Clemson MBA graduate; Corporate Executive (Fortune 50 and Fortune 500 Companies); author of seven books; candidate for the U.S. Senate; candidate for the U.S. House; and Founder and President of Christian Leadership Worldview.

I have been blessed with many various life experiences to be able to share the gospel message and encourage the Christian faithful.

This novel is one of those venues, and I feel overwhelmed to be used in this capacity. In many respects, this book is the culmination of my God-given life journey, and I pray that you are blessed!